Molsey Blount

THE COLONIAL FIRST LADY OF TENNESSEE

Molsey Blount

THE COLONIAL FIRST LADY OF TENNESSEE

From North Carolina to the Frontier of
Tennessee, Her Legacy Continues

NANCY FESSENDEN McENTEE, PhD

Nancy McEntee

Maryville, Tennessee
2018

Mailing Address:
1655 Maple Lane
Greenback, TN 37742

Email: nanflys@yahoo.com

This book is designed to provide accurate and authoritative information with regard to the subject matter covered. This information is given with the understanding that the author is not engaged in rendering legal, professional advice.

Ordering Information:
This book is available from Amazon.com. For bulk purchases, please contact the author.

Book and cover design by Araby Greene.
Cover photo by Nancy Fessenden McEntee.

Molsey Blount: The Colonial First Lady of Tennessee / Nancy Fessenden McEntee, PhD. —2d ed.

1. History / United States / State & Local / South (AL, AR, FL, GA, KY, LA, MS, NC, SC, TN, VA, WV)
2. Biography & Autobiography / Women

Printed in the United States of America

ISBN: 978-1-9858-8779-4

To my sweet husband, Jack—

If Molsey was here, she would be delighted that her story is finally told. She would probably invite you to the Mansion for tea and graciously thank you for your part in bringing her story to life. For the innumerable times you asked me, "When are you going to write that book?" I thank you.

Acknowledgments

In the writing of this book, my greatest debt is to my husband, John Joseph McEntee. This book would not exist if he had not lovingly prodded me into writing Molsey Blount's story. Now that it is finished, he thinks I should write another book.

In researching a historical subject's life, a writer comes in contact with many people that hold a piece of the puzzle or a long disregarded fact about the individual. Early in my journey into the archives and libraries of North Carolina and Tennessee, I visited the Blount Mansion in Knoxville. At that time, David Akin, a staff member, introduced me to the Blount brothers, admitting that he knew little about Mrs. Blount. For his genuine, helpful, and informative support, I am indebted. He guided me through the background of the Blount family and the mansion and answered a myriad of historical questions relating to the Blounts and Knoxville. The current staff of the Blount Mansion was also helpful in supporting Molsey's story.

Other people helped in a greater understanding of Mrs. Blount. To the staff at the Rocky Mount Museum in Piney Flats, Tennessee, and in particular T. J. DeWitt, I offer my sincere gratitude for assisting me in researching the Blounts stay with the Cobbs. The archivist, Candice, at the Lower Cape Fear Historical Society, Inc in Wilmington, N.C., genealogist, Roger Kammerer, Jr of Greenville, and Martha Elmore of East Carolina University's Special Collections deserve my thanks for their efforts in understanding the Blounts of North Carolina. Also, I acknowledge the librarians at the Calvin McClung Historical Collection in Knoxville for their clarity and commitment to accuracy and for their resourceful support. To the University of Tennessee and the family of Crockette Hewlett, thank you for permission to use their historical photos and maps in the completion of this book.

Lastly, a shout out to Tennessee Representative Jimmy Matlock for his suggestion to include the current Tennessee First Lady in this book. With his assistance Crissy Haslam, the current Tennessee First Lady, graciously shared her thoughts on the importance of history and its impact on women. I offer my sincere thank you to both Mrs. Haslam and her assistant, Madeline Walker. Mrs. Haslam's Foreword in this book is a remarkable link between the colonial and current First Ladies.

Contents

Foreword

Tennessee is blessed to have a rich history of influential and interesting people who have helped shape our state and our nation. As the *first* First Lady of Tennessee, Mary "Molsey" Blount contributed tremendously to Tennessee's unique story. Learning about her is an opportunity to better understand our early colonial life and political history.

Mary "Molsey" Blount had little guidance on how to fulfill her role as First Lady, and she helped to lay a foundation for women to lead through service. Her experiences must have been extremely different from being a first lady today, but her example to care for family and community helped to create timeless traditions. To this day, being First Lady is an incredible opportunity to serve, to meet interesting and hardworking people, and to highlight causes that make your community a better place to live.

I hope you enjoy learning about Mary "Molsey" Blount as one of Tennessee's many people to contribute to our unique heritage. We can all be proud to learn from and pay tribute to those who walked before us.

Crissy Haslam

—Crissy Haslam
First Lady of Tennessee

Introduction

Why doesn't anyone know about the life of Mary Blount? Why is she a mystery? Having lived in Blount County, Tennessee, and driven past the William Blount High School and Mary Blount Elementary School in the city of Maryville, Tennessee, it was disheartening to realize Tennessee's first First Lady had been ignored. As the genteel wife of Governor William Blount, her influence and presence in the growth and development of the fledgling state of Tennessee had been overlooked for two centuries, yet she bore witness to some of the most remarkable moments in colonial history. A casual mention of her relationship to Governor Blount, a list of her children (usually inaccurate), and some short biographies about her life and presence at the Blount Mansion in Knoxville, Tennessee, have been the basis of knowledge about Mary Blount, yet her life has shown to be one of great loss, loneliness, courage, and intrigue.

Mary Blount appears historically as an iconic colonial woman. She was born in Wilmington, North Carolina, to an aristocratic family, married during the Revolutionary War, and followed her husband to the Territory South of the River Ohio. She went through what most of the women of that period did—courtship, marriage, birth, and death. Her full life story has somehow escaped the scrutiny of lovers of history. Her silence is now noted, her voice now heard.

In researching the life of Mary Moseley Grainger Blount, it quickly became obvious that history had hidden Mrs. Blount behind her rich, powerful, and politically famous husband, William Blount. Unseen by the formidable volume of letters, papers, and journals left by William and his brothers, Mary Blount stood idle in colonial history. Biographers have applauded, analyzed, and scrutinized her husband's accomplishments for more than two hundred years while ignoring the woman he affectionately called Molsey (pronounced *mall-see*). The historian is never given a direct glimpse of this stately, educated, and admired First Lady of a new territory. Molsey occasionally is revealed, slipping through the comments of an influential land speculator, family member, neighbor, or traveler. Her personality and great beauty can only be surmised by the consistent references to her gracious manners, negotiation skills, household management, entertaining finesse, and the role of wife to her husband of twenty-two years. There is so much more about this colonial woman. Her courage in the face of threatening Indians, her grief in the loss of two children, and her unconditional love of her wandering husband and family live on through reflections and letters of close family members and friends.

The existence of an original thought, word, or image from Molsey Blount is left for future historians, archeologists, anthropologists, and generations to discover. Sadly, extensive research has not exposed a portrait, a diary, a letter, family Bible, or a journal written or drawn by this "dark beauty," as historian Ramsey calls her. Yet her presence remains a part of the Blount legacy—a story of colonial expansion, political intrigue, frontier travel, and Tennessee history. To understand this colonial woman, one must find her in the written comments of her husband and his brothers, see her upbringing and education in the magnificent Blount Mansion in Knoxville, Tennessee, and appreciate her contributions to society in the comments from her neighbors and business friends of her husband.

Often colonial women's voices are unheard, buried in the cacophony of male histories and accomplishments by the belief that their lives were predictable, filled with simple domestic pleasures, and somewhat frivolous. Historians have habitually noted the historical value of women as inferior to men, based on their roles as wife, mother, and household mistress. Historian Mary Beth Norton proposes women of this age were struggling with their own identities, self-esteem, and the denigration of their gender. The question is then asked, Was Molsey like these women? Was she someone to be forgotten? The rich and diverse history of women in the 1700s and, in particular, the women in North Carolina and Tennessee, is slowly being revealed.

This writer proposes that this extraordinary woman was unique for her time. Her apparent shadow in history does not suggest a weakness or a lack of character but a gentleness and aristocratic demeanor of the Governor's lady, or maybe she was the opposite. Maybe she was troubled, or even depressed. A lack of her own words does not indicate a shy, uneducated, or backwoods woman; it simply suggests her need not to share the stage with her famous husband or her respect for a powerful man's imposition on history. Future generations may discover original works by Molsey Blount, contributing to the legacy of a remarkable woman. For now, this book shall act as a herald, holding the door open for further study on Molsey Blount, the colonial First Lady of Tennessee.

The silent voice of Molsey in the historical record was a call to do something bold. Giving meaning and words to her silence was a challenge that was only exceeded by the need to include her in the historical conversation. To include her would mean listening to the world she lived in at the time. Included in her story is her family, traditions, culture, geography, and heritage. Credible evidence has documented the changes in her life and in her family, as well as changes in her environment. Though license was taken in the opening of each chapter, the genesis of each segment "is a true story imagined." Imagined are the first pages of each chapter that allow Molsey to speak to us clearly, something she had not done in history. Completing this biography are unpublished insights into her personality and new details about her life with William Blount.

One cannot meet Molsey Blount without spending time with her husband, William. He overshadows her years of transitions and turmoil. His powerful political position as Governor of the territory that becomes Tennessee, and his questionable practices as a land speculator, Indian agent, and businessman will be questioned by historians for years. Yet his presence in her life is undeniable. Part of her story is his story. Though this is a story about Molsey Blount, it is unavoidable to discuss William, a man who has stood in the historical limelight often. Rest assured, the writer promises only a minimum of discussion about him, focusing this story on the life of Molsey Blount. After all, she was the First Lady of Knoxville and of Tennessee.

1

March 22, 1800—Knoxville, Tennessee

He was gone, forever silenced in this world by his death. His once-strong, gentle hands lay cold and still as his frozen invincible smile faded into the gray shadows of the parlor and her aching heart. Wearily, she leaned against the wall near the doorway, trying to steady herself under the teeming sadness that enveloped her. The elegant mansion felt like a tomb, chilled in the early spring night, crystal chandeliers eclipsed in the moonlight's icy fingers invading the parlor room. Everyone else lay sleeping. Her slave Hagar had left a candle flickering in the parlor, a homing beacon calling to her in her heart's desperate need to once more see her lifelong friend, lover, and husband. Numbed by this loss of that which was more than half of her heart and soul—her husband, William—and trembling weakly from the feverish illness that had been threatening her and their son, she shuffled hesitantly toward the dark wooden coffin. In a day or so, she would see him no more. By then he would be buried beneath mounds of memories and dust, hailed by all within the city he worked to help form, along with the state that proclaimed him a hero. But for now—for a moment at least—he belonged only to her.

An all-consuming distress and grief had left her vaguely aware of the deepest stirrings of loss and the black void growing within her that followed. She had lain abed, already sickened and racked by the passing of her mother just sixteen days before, unable to be with her beloved William when his own life had suddenly fled from him. Her mother's death had gripped her, binding her in crippling distress as she took to her bed, mournfully rocking in the pounding silence of her loss. Her own daughter's fever had shorn away at her resolve even more, adding to the relentless flood of suffering and loss that eroded the worn pathway within her.

Barely able to stand, she had managed to creep in the dark depths of night to the parlor, leaning on the strength of the walls along the hallway. Her bare feet mirrored the naked pain in her soul as the cold hardwood floor whispered of the icy finality of death. Slowly and softly on reluctant, unsteady feet, her body burned from the combined forces of fever and the abysmal emptiness and yearning for her beloved. Molsey struggled for each breath. Grief cruelly clenched her hand, methodically guiding her to shadowed coffin. William was gone forever. He had left so quickly, so unexpectedly; death had been a sudden and unwelcome visitor, robbing her forever of his presence. Death left her emptied of all hope, stealing her purpose for being in this frigid mansion in Tennessee. And this time, out of all the times he had had to leave her alone before, he didn't even say good-bye. He just left, leaving in his wake an insufferable, searing, slicing pain and an insentient soul.

Resting a trembling hand on the polished wood surface of the coffin, Molsey felt a creeping, pervasive fear ooze into her soul.

"Maybe this really didn't happen," she whispered. "Maybe it is part of this fever, this weakness I've been wallowing in. Maybe, just maybe…" Sobs overtook her thoughts and all else. Biting tears blurred the flickering candlelight as they ran in rivulets down her cheeks. She vainly wiped her flushed face with the sleeve of her nightdress, unable to staunch the flow. The room spun dizzily as her grief spilled to the floor, and her body crumpled like crinoline, leaving her lying in the agonizing chains of her breaking heart. At the loss of her life's love, her world came to a crashing end. Her heart would not be comforted or consoled. She lay on the hard floor, imprisoned by the hurtful loss of his abandonment. She ached solely for his return. She longed to embrace her own death.

Time stood frozen in that shrouded silence, broken only by her tears and slowly ebbing sobs. Molsey lay on the cold, unfeeling floor, knowing nothing of hope or her need. Eventually, the discomfort of the darkness began prodding at her, her solitude a persistent monster that gnawed on her emotions, leaving her void of feelings or cares. Without her William, there was nothing that mattered in her world. The voiceless mansion echoed her hollow heart's despair. Where would she go now? Who would be there at the end of her journey? The cruel rains of bitterness and throes of self-pity hung heavily upon her heart like a blanket covering a corpse. And thus she descended into a deep dark cavern of torturous anguish and blinding sorrow.

Thus began the desolate and forlorn journey of Mary "Molsey" Grainger Blount following the death of her husband, William Blount, the former "Governor of the Territory South of the River Ohio." Married for twenty-two years, most of which were lived apart from her husband due to the ravages of war and other responsibilities he had taken upon himself, Molsey was left with six of her children in Knoxville and one child who resided in North Carolina with relatives. Her mother, Mary, had lived for years with her and her family in the Blount Mansion. She had been buried sixteen days prior to William's death, having died from a bilious fever. Only the slaves remained with Molsey in the mansion on the knoll. Her brother-in-law Willie(pronounced *why-lee*), a resident of Knoxville, was in Nashville attending to family business.

Her children—Louisa (eighteen), Billy (sixteen), Richard (eleven), Jacob (nine), Barbara (eight), and Eliza (five)—learned of their father's death the day after he died. Their grief visceral and bewildering, the children turned to the family slaves for comfort as their mother, prostrate with grief, returned to her bed. Several days passed before Uncle Willie returned from Nashville to reassure the children that they would be cared for and their futures secured.

The future was not so clear for William Blount's widow. He had not left a will. Not only had the mansion been deeded to his brother Willie to avoid foreclosure, he had left no instructions regarding the dispersal of his personal property. Willie, his personal secretary on the frontier, was therefore left as sole owner of the mansion and all its contents and outbuildings. William's death ensured continued ownership of the Blount Mansion by a Blount, but it was not left to Molsey. She would continue to reside in the mansion for another two years, restrained by her brother-in-law Willie's authority and legal right to the property.

William's death came as a shock to his wife, his family, the community, his political and business foes and friends, and to the new State of Tennessee. Though he had suffered off and on throughout his life with malaria, yellow fever, piles, and sundry injuries, his health prior to his death was unremarkable. Preceding his death on March 21, William Blount had attended to his oldest son Billy, who had been violently ill with bilious fever: a fever caused by a liver disorder, as noted in a colonial tome on illnesses. Apparently Billy was seriously ill, yet Molsey was unable to attend to him. Her mother, Mary Grainger, had just died of a fever and had been hurriedly buried. Another child, Louisa, was recovering from a similar illness, culminating with Molsey's need to be confined a day or two in bed. Death and illness ran rampant through the mansion.

John Summerville, a confidential agent of William, describes, in volume 3 of the *John Gray Blount Papers* (Masterson 1965), Blount's death in the mansion:

> On the evening of Saturday the 15. Instant after reading newspapers in the piazza 'till it was so late he could not distinguish a letter, was taken very suddenly with a violent chill in 1/2 hour after drinking his coffee, (at which he felt as well as he ever did) to this succeeded a violent fever & that night & the next day he was

delirious...Monday & Tuesday he appeared so well that no doubt was entertained of his immediate recovery, but before Wednesday morning (for that night he felt so well that he would suffer no person to sit up with him) he caught a second cold which seized upon his lungs...he was blistered a second time.

Summerville attended his friend on the twenty-first and noted another relapse and another recovery. Thinking Blount was recovering again, Summerville was dispirited as Blount's life began to ebb. Summerville realized that Blount's speech was impaired, denoting a possible stroke. Blount seemed disoriented and slurred his words. His friend, in a later letter recorded in volume 3 of the *John Gray Blount Papers* (Masterson 1965), writes to William's brother Thomas in North Carolina:

He turned his eyes upon me as I leaned over him wetting his lips, watching every breath that he breathed...looked steadfastly at me some minutes, tried to speak...and finding that he could not, he turned away his head...his eyes immediately filled and the tears rolled in large drops down his cheeks for several minutes, and at 21 minutes after 5...he breathed his last.

Molsey was faced with the deaths, only sixteen days apart, of two of the people she loved most—her mother and her husband. Her mother, often referred to as Mrs. Grainger, had lived with the Blounts off and on since the early 1780s. She had provided love, wisdom, and companionship to her daughter through the decades of emptiness left by Blount's travels and business arrangements. Now her mother, recently buried, was taken from her life, along with her husband. Louisa, Molsey's oldest daughter, provided some comfort but was also stunned by her father's death. Nancy, Molsey's daughter raised by William's brother and sister, lived in North Carolina. It would be months before Nancy would arrive in Knoxville. Family slaves, such as Hagar or Sall, would be on hand to provide for the daily needs of the remaining family in the mansion.

Admired by friends and acquaintances in Knoxville, considered an example of elegance and grace on the Tennessee frontier, Molsey, at the age of thirty-nine, became a widow, facing a future of uncertainty and sadness. Where had this great love gone? Where had it all begun?

2

October 1765—
Wilmington, North Carolina

Molsey's mother, Mary, was weeping once more. Fear gripped the young Molsey, seeing her mother sitting among the shadows in her bedroom, her body shaking with sobs and tears flowing unchecked down her face. Slowly, ever so slowly, little four-year-old Molsey haltingly stepped foot into the room. Chickens clucked to each other outside the room's window. She fixed her gaze on the red-and-blue quilted bedcover, her mother's fingers stroking the wrinkled cotton surface. Unknown and unwelcome tendrils of fear and panic overtook her tiny frame. The palpable presence of her mother's agony riveted Molsey to the braided rug, halting her approach. What was wrong? To her little-girl mind, her mother's tears were foreign, something dangerous and threatening. Molsey was aware that her mother was expecting another baby brother or sister for her to play with, and before now that awareness had always brightened her mother's face with warm smiles.

Her mother's gaze broke through the wall of paralyzing fear as she looked up to Molsey and reached out her arms for her. Molsey sped to her mother, throwing herself into the pregnant woman's embrace. Her mother's tears lessened as she stroked her daughter's hair and whispered comforting words of love in her little ear. Lifting Molsey's chin, she lovingly and gently kissed her daughter, telling her it would all be okay. Unable to comprehend the anguish behind her mother's words, Molsey held tight to her mother's thick waist and began to rock. She instinctually felt something wasn't right as she peeked up into her mother's tear-streaked face, searching for a smile. Slowly her mother wiped at her red-rimmed eyes, then her nose, before straightening her hair. Setting Molsey on the floor before her, she attempted to tell her little girl something that Molsey struggled to understand. Her father, Caleb, had died. Did that mean he wouldn't be coming come home today? Where did he go? Her young child's mind raced to try and learn what *death* meant while she hugged her mother close, trying to comfort and console her for whatever was causing her so much obvious hurt and pain.

Her older brothers, Caleb Jr. and Cornelius, were different too. They were eerily quiet at suppertime. Everyone was quiet—too quiet. The only other person in the family, her two-year-old brother William, was his usual self, obliviously playful and babbling. It comforted her that he could play with her as if everything were the same as ever.

Her elder brothers were impatient with her and seemed to ignore her, telling her over and over that it would be all right, but it wasn't all right. Her mother kept weeping, and her brothers impatiently brushed her questions away. Her aunts and uncles arrived, making her even more curious with her questions that had no answers and leaving her alone with William. Everyone seemed concerned with her mother, heavily pregnant and in obvious distress. Molsey was tucked in bed early that night, something she would learn to do for herself whenever anything in her world became too much for her to handle.

⁓꧁꧂⁓

Caleb Grainger's little girl was bereft of a father, who also left behind a pregnant wife and three more children. He had been the backbone of the family and an influential resident of Wilmington. The town had been an important part of the Grainger family's life, along with the development of the low country of North Carolina; Grainger roots were deep there.

Wilmington, a port city, was a British town under the authority of King George III in the 1760s. The town relied heavily on its lumber industry and naval stores. By 1763, the Lower Cape Fear district, which included Wilmington, boasted 6,284 people, many of whom were slaves. The area consisted of marshlands, low flat beds of grass, blue herons, sandpipers, small forests of pine and deciduous trees, gently rolling hills of sand, and oyster beds; the smell of salt water permeated the breezes. New settlers clustered close to Wilmington or around Brunswick to the south. The main road between Wilmington and the new capital of New Bern, North Carolina, to the north was made up of dirt and sand, winding its way toward the capital's governmental seat. South of Wilmington, Fort Johnston squatted on the west bank of the Cape Fear River, an uncertain defense against the French, Spanish, and pirates that often threatened the coast.

Wilmington, the largest town in New Hanover County, attracted settlers from South Carolina, Barbados, and the British Isles. By 1749, the city had become an excellent place to engage in waterborne trades, boasting a twenty-six-foot-wide wharf—an excellent port for small boats and the burgeoning colonial shipping business. Over the next three years another wharf was constructed at the end of Market Street. It wasn't long before the town imposed laws on Wilmington businesses and citizens. A man was only allowed to anchor his boat to the wharf for twenty-four hours, and all able-bodied men had to help maintain the unpaved streets. Dogs weren't allowed to roam the streets, and all runaways or strays were shot. In those colonial times, disease ran rampart, and cures were uncertain and unknown, making stray animals a reasonable threat to the health and welfare of the citizens. A trash collector was required, and citizens had to purchase two fire buckets per family to assist in quelling any fires. Wilmington was more contemporary than most cities, purchasing a fire engine in 1745. Approximately 4,200 people had settled in the Lower Cape Fear region by 1755 under the rule of England's monarchy, which believed such colonists were obliged to remain loyal to the king.

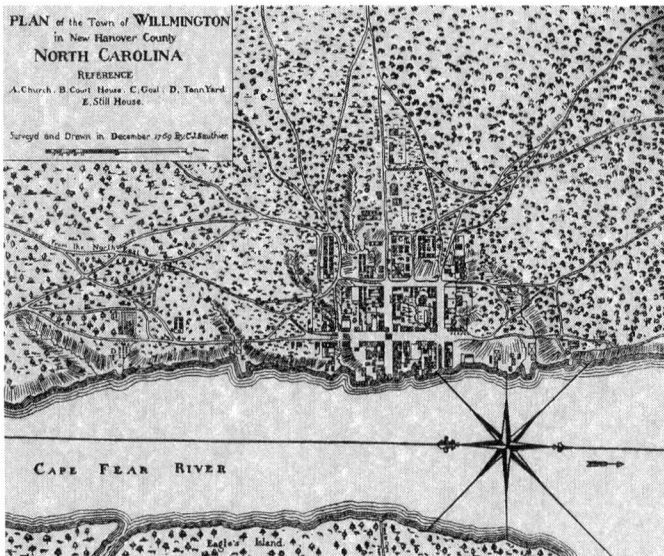

PLAN of the Town of WILLMINGTON
in New Hanover County
NORTH CAROLINA
REFERENCE
A.Church B.Court House C.Goal D. Tann Yard
E. Still House.

Surveyd and Drawn in December 1769 ByC.J.Sauthier

CAPE FEAR RIVER

Eagles Island

An early map of Wilmington, North Carolina, drawn in 1769. Molsey was born in Wilmington in 1761, living there until she married William Blount in 1778.

By the mid-eighteenth century, the Graingers of Wilmington, North Carolina (originally named Newton), were a prominent, semi-aristocratic British family. They stood proud of their English heritage and their successes in the colony of North Carolina, including their business accomplishments in lumber, tar, turpentine, and as local merchants. Settling in what would become known as the Cape Fear district of coastal North Carolina, Joshua Grainger (Molsey's grandfather) was a Quaker, merchant, justice of the peace and landowner. Born in 1702, he had immigrated to the British colonies as a young man. He met and married Elizabeth Ann Toomer in 1722, a twenty-year-old young lady from Newtown. Eleven years later, in 1733, Joshua Grainger, James Wimble, Michael Dyer, and John Watson joined together in obtaining grants to lay out what would become the future town of Wilmington. These city founders then proceeded to sell lots and survey streets. Joshua Grainger had surveyed a large lot on the north side of Market Street, close to Wilmington's markets, church, and seaport. He is credited with founding the shipyard at the foot of Church Street in Wilmington, a shipyard that is still active today, a popular port from which the white oak timbers produced in the area were shipped.

Molsey's grandparents, Joshua and Elizabeth Grainger, bore three children: Joshua Jr., born in 1723; Caleb, born in 1725; and Ann, born about 1727. Molsey's grandmother died at the age of thirty-nine in 1741, and her grandfather died in 1746, leaving substantial land and profits to his sons Joshua and Caleb. Ann did not receive land simply because women could not legally own property during those colonial times. There is little known about Joshua or Ann Grainger. Molsey would never know her father's brother, Joshua, who died in 1763, when she was just two years old. Caleb, the second son, was Molsey's father. Ann married John Dubois, and the date of her death is unknown.

Caleb Grainger, Molsey's father, was born in Wilmington in 1725. He was respected, well liked, industrious, and actively involved in the governing of Wilmington. Described as a man of culture and letters, he inherited his father's lands along with his business skills. Caleb continued to serve his community, county, and country throughout his life. In 1750, he married the widow Mary Salter Baker and remained in Wilmington, North Carolina. His accomplishments included holding the New Hanover County office of sheriff in 1754, functioning as an inn-holder and owning large portions of land. Governor Dobbs, the governor of North Carolina from 1754 to 1765, described him as a "gentleman of good fortune in the province." Caleb Grainger was one of the first eight Aldermen of Wilmington and a state representative in 1747. As a Lieutenant Colonel, he served in the Innes regiment to Virginia in 1754, and as Captain of a military company, he was sent on an expedition to Crown Point, New York, in 1756 under Major Dobbs, the governor's son.

Mary Salter Baker, Molsey's mother, came from an affluent family and was well educated. She brought to her marital union several lots on Front Street in Wilmington and an inheritance of twenty pounds from a citizen named Alexander Duncan. Her marriage of fifteen years to Caleb produced five children, all living to adulthood: Caleb Jr., born about 1747; Cornelius Harnett, born about 1750; Mary Moseley, born 1761; William, born 1763; and John, born 1765 or 1766. The exact birth dates of Molsey's siblings vary depending on historical sources. Birth certificates were not required in colonial North Carolina, leaving historians and genealogists to sometimes disagree on the exact date by a year or two. Molsey's year of birth, however, is uncontested. She was born in 1761, as indicated in the inscription on her grave. Still, after extensive research, the exact date of her birth remains incomplete, void of the precise month and day she was born.

Molsey's oldest brother was named after their father. Caleb Jr. followed in the footsteps of his father's military career, serving as a Regulator in a local battle that occurred in the future Alamance County, north of current-day Greensboro, North Carolina. The Battle of Alamance was one of several precursors to the coming revolution, though this battle was based on problems centered on taxation and local control. In the end, British Governor Tryon settled these concerns by utilizing redcoats, causing several deaths. Caleb Grainger Jr. also served as a Major in the American Revolution in the First North Carolina Line from February 5 to April 1777. He wed a widow by the name of Mary/Sarah Haskell during the revolution in February of 1779, one year after Molsey and William Blount married.

Cornelius Harnett Grainger was born in 1750. Mary and Caleb Grainger delighted in naming their children after famous individuals. This tradition was meaningful to Molsey, as the reader will see, since her own children were also christened for famous and popular individuals. Cornelius Harnett, for whom they named their son, was popular among the citizens of Wilmington, serving the community as a farmer, merchant, and statesman. Instrumental in the defense of Wilmington during the Revolutionary War, he was chairman of the Sons of Liberty and a delegate to the Constitutional Convention. Harnett was also a close family friend of the Graingers, sharing their political ideology, summer vacations, and as it turned out, he was also familiar with Molsey's future husband William Blount, and his family. Named after a famous war hero and politician, Cornelius Harnett Grainger served in the revolution in the North Carolina Regiment, later moving to South Carolina.

Edward Moseley, a friend of Molsey's father, drew this early map of the Cape Fear area in 1733, prior to her birth in 1761. Molsey's (note spelling) nickname is similar; as her middle name was Moseley.

Mary Moseley Grainger was born in Wilmington, North Carolina, in 1761, the year a horrible hurricane swept through, lasting for four days and destroying much of the Cape Fear area. Molsey, a colloquial simplification of her middle name, was the familiar, endearing nickname she was known by throughout her life, by family as well as friends. She was named for Edward Moseley, a notable lawyer and surveyor of North Carolina who created the Moseley map of North Carolina that was printed in 1733. He was renowned for his impartial justice and his hatred of oppressive government, often noted in the history of North Carolina. Another reason for her nickname is that Molsey was one of many Marys in her family. Her mother, sisters-in-law, and several aunts and cousins were also named Mary. Later, William Blount would call her Ms. Grainger during their courtship, followed affectionately by *Molly* during their early married years. Today, the names Grainger and Moseley can be found throughout Eastern North Carolina: Grainger Point, Grainger Road, Moseley Creek.

William Grainger was born two years after Molsey. He married Susannah Smith in 1786 and moved to Craven County, North Carolina. Shortly after their marriage, he died in 1788, at the age of twenty-two. There isn't a lot known of his personal history. By the time of his death, Molsey had been married for several years and was the mother of four children. He left her son, William Grainger Blount, his property in Wilmington upon his death in 1788. The boy was only four years old at the time.

Molsey's youngest brother remains a mystery. Molsey's father, Caleb, died in 1765 or 1766, leaving behind a pregnant wife. Most historians agree that the baby was born after Caleb's death, around 1766, and was probably named John. The information concerning John is contained in a codicil to his father's will. Apparently, as Molsey's father was dying, he was aware of this new addition to his family and wanted to provide for that child in his last will and testament.

Caleb and Mary Grainger raised their children in typical British colonial fashion. Their children were educated in the aristocratic manners necessary to demonstrate civility, courtesy, and etiquette. They had little knowledge of the world outside of Wilmington. Elders and family members possibly told stories of pirates off the coast of Wilmington or sailors' tales, but for the most part, their formal learning came directly from their parents and other relatives. The Grainger boys likely attended a local school, whereas Molsey would not have attended such a school.

There are few records concerning Molsey's younger years. Historical comments state she was educated, well read, and trained to be a young lady. To have won the heart of gentleman and businessman William Blount infers that she was all that. It is most likely she learned her letters, studied the Bible, and learned to play the piano in her home. In affluent colonial homes, education for young females consisted of writing and arithmetic, along with the occasional Latin and, often, music. She would most certainly have studied these rudimentary educational subjects.

Molsey basked in the attention her brothers showered upon her. As the only girl in a family of four boys, it wouldn't be unusual for her to by teased and taunted but also protected and spoiled by her family. Having become a part of the elite in Wilmington, her father accumulated great wealth, mainly in land, slaves, and personal property. The Grainger family owned three homes. Historian Hewlett states in *Between the Creeks: A History of Masonborough Sound, 1735–1970* (Wilmington Press Co. 1971) that they "had a home on the Black River and a place called 'Sans Souci.'" Their third residence, known as the Masonborough Plantation, was much more than a "summer place on the sound." History records that it was "a fine place for the boys, where they could sail a boat and go swimming and fishing." The Sans Souci residence, often detailed throughout Grainger history, was a plantation on the Northeast Cape Fear River north of Wilmington. North of the Smith Creek, this plantation was near Cornelius Harnett's plantation, the Hilton, and other prominent Wilmington residents' summer homes.

The Masonborough Plantation was the Grainger summer residence, a house built on Grainger land south of Wilmington, which is between today's Whiskey Creek and Hewlett's Creek. The original deed recorded 320 acres, purchased on August 1, 1758, for two hundred pounds. Lands surrounding the home were filled with lacy dogwoods in the spring and goldenrod in the summer. Abundant species of wildlife such as foxes, turkeys, squirrels, opossums, and a variety of waterfowl made themselves comfortable in those woods. The naming of the residence is disputed throughout various historical documents. Most researchers agree that it had something to do with Caleb Grainger's membership in the Free Masons. During the summer months, Masonborough Plantation provided for endless joyful family gatherings, for outings like swimming and fishing. Mary and Caleb frequently entertained Masonic Lodge brothers, politicians, and relatives in this home.

On several occasions, a young man by the name of Thomas Godfrey was a guest at Masonborough Plantation. He had just recently arrived in Wilmington and met Caleb while working at an export firm. Godfrey yearned to be a poet and playwright and discovered that Masonborough offered the ideal tranquility and quiet needed for inspiration. It was there that he was able to reach his goals in writing drama and poetry. In honor of his time spent with the Graingers, he penned a poem entitled *Masonborough*, a lyric poem lauding the beauty, creation, and breezes of the home. Unfortunately, at the age of twenty-three, he was seized with a violent fever and died at Masonborough on July 25, 1763.

Today, the Masonborough Plantation is but a memory, having decayed over the centuries, dispersed among the Atlantic winds. In 1971, the author Hewlett wrote of the existence of a small cottage, the Anderson Cottage, still standing on the plantation property. It is believed to be the last remaining structure from the time the Graingers owned the property. This cottage is described in *Between the Creeks: A History of Masonborough Sound 1735–1970* (Wilmington Press Colk 1971) as having a "high pitched roof with a three-foot overhang in front, affording shelter to the entrance and allowing dormitory space above, reached by a flight of outside stairs. On the first floor are two rooms measuring ten by thirteen feet in size." The small cottage was roofed with wooden shingles blanketed in lichen and moss. Beside this small cottage was a huge live oak, possibly a tree that had stood sentinel since the 1760s.

When Molsey was just four years old, her beloved father died. The Masonborough Plantation then fell quiet, standing empty for years. Eventually, it was deeded to her mother who sold it in 1772 for "the benefit of her sons," as directed in Caleb's will (*Last Will and Testament* 1765). Only forty years old at the time of his death, Caleb left behind an expectant wife and four minor children. He had been a profitable planter, innkeeper, landowner, loving husband and father, and a respected esquire. He bequeathed lands and instructions to his sons while willing Molsey two slaves, furniture, a lot in Wilmington, and household items in his will. These items would become legally hers upon her seventeenth birthday or her marriage, both of which occurred during her seventeenth year.

Mary, her mother, would never remarry, focusing the remainder of her life in caring for Molsey and her brothers. Caleb had left her lands, slaves, and a few profitable businesses. With the support and aid of her family, Mary maintained her family in comfort and stability. Molsey watched as her mother developed into the strong sole head of her household, a sound example for the role she herself would have to assume in her own future.

3

February 1776—
Wilmington, North Carolina

"Only seventy Loyalists soldiers were killed—only seventy!" shouted Uncle Joseph as he hurriedly shut the door behind him and tossed his tricornered hat on the table.

Molsey's mother bustled about him, peppering her uncle, who had just returned from the courthouse, with questions. Wringing her faded blue apron and twisting its rough edges in her work-worn hands, her mother listened anxiously to every word that spilled from his lips as he reported on the battle at Widow Moore's Creek Bridge. Molsey tightly clutched the stair railings to quell the mounting fear within her as she overheard the fervid conversation. Had her brothers been in that battle? Where was Caleb? Why wasn't Cornelius here? These questions and more milled through her turbid mind. The details from her uncle did little to ease her anxious heart and unsteady thoughts. Her world was dissolving before her eyes, disfigured by something she couldn't and didn't want to understand, didn't want to think about. Her beloved Wilmington was being inextricably drawn into this fever for independence.

Uncle Joseph paused for breath before going on with his report, pointing out the ominous fact that Moore's Creek Bridge was but eighteen miles north of Wilmington. This battle at the bridge was too close to her home both in distance and the fact that two of her beloved brothers were fighting in it. Battling for the American cause was risky, but the British oppression was even worse. Her whole family had taken up the new patriot flag, losing many of their friends to the British Loyalists.

The British redcoats had marched with the North Carolina Highland Scots Loyalists to do battle with the North Carolina Patriots. Through the ravaging losses on both sides, the Patriots had emerged the winners. Uncle Joseph voiced his belief that the British also meant to march to Wilmington for a planned rendezvous with a British naval expedition. Molsey's mind was laced with recent memories of when she had overheard her mother speak heatedly of the shared resentments toward the Crown that some of their friends and relatives held in common, speaking of how the colony of North Carolina might join with other colonies in a declaration of independence. So much conflict and consternation was going on within the confines of her small town. She recalled with resignation how just a few years ago the seaport of Wilmington had been closed to British trade. In her teens now, she could only visualize in her mind's eye what it was like for the women of Wilmington to toss away their precious English tea just a few years ago, refusing to buy more. At fifteen, she was beginning to realize the high price such battle for independence demanded. The Redcoats had been driven away from Wilmington, no longer able to flirt with her. Dashed were her cherished dreams and hopes of becoming a British lady.

Once her uncle left the home, having reassured her mother that the British would not be coming to Wilmington anytime soon, the peal of the townsman's bell began to ring out, calling the citizens of Wilmington to gather on Market Street. The bell's pealing ring reminded her of how the bell would ring at St. James Episcopal Church when the rector signaled a wedding, a death, a meeting, a victory, and, of course, a church service. The friendly song of the bell had been a constant her whole life. The memories of the bell recalled to her how as a small girl, she had spent Sundays sitting on the hardwood bench of pew 10 with her mother and father, a pew specifically reserved for her family and shared with John London's family. She recalled how her father had patiently pointed out to her the beautiful artwork entitled *Ecce Homo*, a portrait of Christ painted by Francisco Pacheco. The tail he spun about how the Spanish ship *Fortuna* had lost a great battle, leaving the painting to be discovered in the captain's cabin, was one she never tired of hearing. That painting still hung on the church wall.

St. James Church (Colonial)

Commenced 1751

The original building of St. James Episcopal Church. Molsey's father rented Pew 10 in this church when she was young. The church was closed during the Revolutionary War when the Blounts married.

All her life, she had attended many a beautiful wedding in the sanctuary of the small church, her head filled with daydreams of the day she would also be wed there. St. James Episcopal Church, close to the corners of Market and Fourth Street, had always been a comfort and source of stability to the young Molsey.

Now the church stood vacant and abandoned, identified as part and parcel of the English government. The Reverend Willis was believed to be a Loyalist, a member of the clergy preaching for England's cause. Managing to push aside her reminiscences, she strode hurriedly with her mother and younger brother, her thoughts turning from uncertainty to the hope of seeing her other siblings at the called-for gathering in town. She grasped the hand of her ten-year-old brother John, who embarrassingly shook her off, indignantly proclaiming he was too old for her help. The cloudy, blustery afternoon mirrored her own milieu of confusion and concern as her long sweeping hair whipped and twisted in the insistent fingers of the wind. The well-worn wool skirt that she had overdyed in indigo clung to her legs, slowing her pace, entangling with her thoughts and hopes. Worry hastened beside her. She began to run, eager to flee the invading fears of her thoughts, yearning for someone to reassure her and shield her from what she was certain would be an obstacle to her happiness and a stumbling block to innocence. For more than a year now, North Carolinians had stubbornly resisted the oppression of King George. The Battle at Moore's Creek was another unwanted reminder of the valor and patriotic enthusiasm shared by Molsey's neighbors and relatives. She loathed fighting and bickering. She just wanted it all to go away.

～ℰℓℓ℘℘～

Prerevolutionary years would have been difficult for the teenaged Molsey. She had grown up without a father and with a preoccupied mother. Many transitions and changes crowded her adolescence. Summers at Masonborough had ceased long ago after her father's death. Her oldest brother had left home, married, and now lived with his wife, Mary Haskell. Cornelius had also married, leaving Molsey at home with William and John, her younger brothers. Her aunt Ann Grainger Jewkes had lost her first husband and had remarried in 1773. Often Ann and Aunt Elizabeth visited the family, sharing current family news, tidbits of gossip, and town happenings.

For as far back as Molsey could recall, Wilmington and her beloved North Carolina had been fighting the British, both in words and actions. English rule was dispensed by royal governors appointed by King George. If it wasn't the British the were squabbling with her neighbors and family, it was the last remaining Tuscarora Indians fighting the English over their remaining lands. Gov. Josiah Martin had been forced to flee the capital in New Bern, North Carolina, in 1775, heading to Fort Johnson, ten miles south of Molsey's former summer home, the Masonborough Plantation. As the Patriots burned Fort Johnson, Martin escaped again, fleeing to a British warship. Subsequently, Wilmington citizens organized the Wilmington Independent Company and the Wilmington Artillery Company in defense of their town.

All this discord and contention proved unnerving to the young lady. Surely war with England was on the horizon. Cornelius Harnett had become the Sam Adams of North Carolina, rallying colonists to unite in resistance against the imposed Stamp Act and other British policies. As the leader of the Sons of Liberty, Harnett headed the citizens of North Carolina in forming a provincial congress. Most likely Molsey overheard the plans of this new government, led by Harnett as its president. By August 1, 1776, North Carolina had joined the other colonies in a formal Declaration of Independence.

Many citizens of Wilmington struggled with deciding to remain loyal to the king, or joining up with the Patriots. The Grainger family chose the path to independence. Suddenly, Molsey found herself and her family no longer British. Recognized traitors by the Crown, defense of their homeland became critical. She watched her brothers Caleb and William as they joined up with the North Carolina militia, marching off to war in defense of their right to freedom and self-governance. Caleb Grainger Jr. earned the rank of Major and served in the Third Regiment for North Carolina. William Grainger's service was noted in history, yet he was not an officer in the militia. Both brothers managed to survive the Revolutionary War.

With the banishment of English goods in Wilmington, its citizens had to produce their own fabric, foods, and clothing. Molsey's comfortable life had been forever changed. She was impacted not only by the violence of the war surrounding her but by the absence of men as well. Without a father and her brothers off to war, the balance of work shifted at home out of sheer necessity. With slaves to continue the hard manual labor, Molsey and her mother underwent a shift in the typical roles assigned to women. The colonial ideal of woman's work, with certain tasks clearly assigned to women and others considered improper, faced a crisis. Prior to the revolution, men and women had accepted and subtly played out the belief that women were inferior to men. Norton notes in *Liberty's Daughters: The Revolutionary Experience of American Women, 1750–1800* (Little, Brown and Company 1980) that "most of the white women who lived in pre-revolutionary America displayed a sense of low self-esteem, having very limited conceptions of themselves and their roles, and habitually denigrating their sex in general." The long-term effects of war opened up opportunities for women to gain a better sense of themselves and their roles as women, creating new trends in the way they thought and behaved. Genteel women like Mrs. Grainger and her daughter had been raised to display the "proper" characteristics of colonial femininity. Norton also states that women were "delicate, pure, tender, irritable, affectionate, flexible and patient...chaste, modest, cheerful, sympathetic, affable and emotional." Lacking a husband or a father in the home, it was only natural a well-developed autonomy and independence became the new norm for women in the Grainger household.

During times of war, it is not uncommon for individuals to turn to religion and a strong spiritual faith for solace and comfort. The historical record is silent concerning this aspect of the Grainger family, except for the fact that Molsey's father had a family pew reserved in St. James Episcopal Church. One could argue that this practice would not guarantee a family's faith, yet ownership of a church pew in colonial Wilmington indicates that the Grainger family participated in the common practice of collective worship and an experience with God. Most colonial men and women believed that God's will was something one had to be resigned to in their lives. Reaching a place of contentment with one's life no matter what happened was the goal.

40

As a widow Mrs. Grainger modeled to Molsey, a life as described by Norton set to "extend beyond the boundaries of the standard feminine sphere." When Molsey's father died, her mother was forced to take on more administrative responsibilities and tasks involving the procurement of food and clothing, as well as supervising all domestic help and slaves. Ultimately, those Revolutionary War years effectively disrupted the previously accepted standards of a woman's lack of autonomy. Molsey would find herself in need of these personal traits in her future life as the wife of a governor.

As her mother took on more responsibilities for the family, she also attempted to contribute to helping neighbors and relatives. The escalation of the war for independence exposed colonial women to the politics of war, as well its battles. They were active, along with their neighbors, in boycotting British goods and other items taxed by England. Unfortunately, the teachers and merchants who remained loyal to King George left Wilmington, leaving its residents relying on their own ingenuity or doing without. Mrs. Grainger did her best to keep life as normal as possible for her children. Molsey's education on etiquette and the finer points of becoming a proper lady continued. She learned that it was impolite for young women to lean on another's chair. And Mary Norton suggests (*Liberty's Daughters: Looking Forward, Looking Backward* (Little, Brown and Company 1980) that women knew not to "walk too closely to another when strolling out of doors." She continued playing her piano, studying her letters, and reading such books as the popular *On the Sublime* by Longinus.

She also couldn't help noticing that several of her young friends were already married. Many, in fact, were married at the age of thirteen or fourteen, a customary practice when one's life span was limited to four or five decades. Wisely, Molsey had been well-taught concerning the strict standards imposed on wealthy young women with regard to marriage. Courting behavior was designed to protect the young couple from engaging in too intimate a relationship before marriage. Chaperones were required if the

41

couple roamed from under the noses of the family. Any open display of touching or kissing was forbidden. Andrew Gardner relates in *Courtship, Sex, and the Single Colonist* that even with these precautions, "transgressions were bound to occur."

Secondly, parents were involved in marital decision making. This involvement helped to prevent a girl from giving up her virginity on impulse or making a bad choice in a husband. If a colonial girl decided to violate these rules of propriety, it lessened her chances of securing a good husband in the future. A double standard existed regarding sexual involvement, and the woman alone carried the burden of careless behaviors. Therefore, most young ladies Molsey's age were very aware of the judgmental and strict standards of behavior; "they adhered so carefully to strict standards of behavior." When it was her turn to be courted, it became a collective decision, not an individual one.

Choosing the right husband or wife was critical to upper-class colonists. Colonial law was clear. Upon a marriage, all the wife's possessions became the husband's. A wife was forbidden by law to own property in her own name. If she were divorced, she could not even claim her own children. Therefore, a woman in the eighteenth century had to choose her future husband wisely. Mrs. Grainger knew that from experience. She had been widowed, all the marital lands and homes passing to her sons, not to her. Everything that Molsey inherited from her father would belong to her future husband.

Another consideration for Molsey regarding a future husband was financial stability. It was imperative she find a suitable man, one with prestige, influence, money, and possibly land. Basing a marriage on economics alone was the norm in colonial genteel North Carolina. To base a marriage on love was an alternative, but the emphasis on finances was more common. The Grainger family remained prominent in the North Carolina war efforts, politics, and the economics in Wilmington throughout the Revolutionary War. The man Molsey married would have to be a gentleman, someone well-educated and esteemed in North Carolina, ideally someone who would also love and care for her.

In 1778, Molsey turned seventeen. The Revolutionary War had spread its tentacles throughout the colonies, covering it like a blanket of cold, muddy sea water. Colonial towns were drenched in musket fire, and soldiers froze at Valley Forge from lack of shoes and coats. Wilmington was under constant threat from Governor Martin's attempts to regain control over North Carolina. Her life as a child had come to an end. She took over the responsibility of her younger brothers, and more household tasks were assigned for her to oversee. She had learned to cook, manage the house slaves, oversee some of the food production, weave, spin, and sew. Embroidered mourning pieces had become popular at that time, something she would have made, embellishing her work with weeping willows and decorative urns. Without English goods, *homemade* was the term that described the Grainger's ability to provide food, drink, medicine, fuel, clothing, and shelter for themselves.

With several family members serving in political or military positions, the Grainger reputation of graciousness and congeniality provided by the women of the household was one which allowed for traveling merchants, military officers, land speculators, and businessmen to frequently be entertained at Mrs. Grainger's home. The ever-popular and well-liked Cornelius Harnett visited often, bringing with him men of nobility and power. One of these visitors was a gentleman serving as paymaster to the North Carolina Regiments, William Blount of Craven County.

4

Summer 1777—
Wilmington, North Carolina

He halted the carriage in the shade beneath a solitary pine tree. The carriage's other passenger, Molsey, did her best to quell her anticipation, quivering in spite of the stifling humidity. The tall black horse, Bell, anxiously pawed at the ground, stirring up the dirt in her obvious eagerness to keep moving while the older horse, Bob, relaxed stolidly, completely at ease, head down, his hide rippling beneath the harness in response to the bite of yet another horsefly. Molsey couldn't keep from holding her breath in the expectation and hope that this stopping of the carriage indicated he had something to say, something she struggled mightily to sit still long enough to hear. The seething, hot, humid breeze from the marshes added to both her discomfort and her impatient waiting. Her fingers twisted nervously among the ribbons of her bonnet as it lay in her lap, and she nibbled at her lower lip. The heat disallowed the possibility of donning the bonnet again. Awakening to the awkwardness of her fumbling among the bonnet ribbons, she so wished he would stop rearranging the reins in his hands. She swore her heart was pounding louder than the katydids. Why was he so silent?

Mr. William Blount had managed to completely ensnare her heart, leaving her featherbrained and faint of heart. Every minute detail—the way he walked, the strength of his hands, and the gentleness mirrored in his eyes—enchanted her every fiber. Each minute of the day was filled with wondering if he would show up at the house or if he would return safe from the battles that devastated her homeland. This war, this terrible Revolutionary War, made it so difficult for her to imagine a future, and it often invaded her sleep with horrific nightmares. But when William was there, standing by her side, that world seemed miles and miles away, in another time and place. Remembrances of his first kiss burning on her young cheek filled her with hours of longing and daydreaming.

Her heart never failed to thrill with the way he called her Ms. Grainger, his voice covering her like a warm bath and burning through her like explosive fireworks. His eyes whispered multitudes of silent secrets, the motion and touch of his hands were never anything other than full of care and gentleness. The strength of his confidence and focus as he guided her into his carriage lingered in her senses like the smell of a sweet magnolia tarrying on the breeze. Maybe this is what love actually felt like. She had thought she had been in love before; now she knew it had been nothing more than love dressed up in a naïve girl's silly wishes. She was sixteen now, almost a spinster, and he was only twelve years older—perfect. William was a well-educated, prosperous, single gentleman, and most importantly, he was with her.

His last visit had lasted far too briefly for her. She had to admit to herself that all his visits were too brief. She could never get enough of his time, his thoughts, and his dreams. He hung on every movement of her fingers as they danced over the piano, wrapping him in her music while she was thrilled with the how he expertly played with her emotions. Happiness, entwined with delight, longing, excitement, and laughter danced in her mind. They had met...when? She gazed down at her hands, breathed in deeply, and told herself that it seemed like they had always known each other. All she knew now was that she wanted to spend forever with him. She thought—she hoped—he wanted the same.

The silence of waiting was deafening as she sat nervously beside William. The warm, wet humidity wrapped each of them in quiet wonder. Sweaty dark curls clung to her cheeks. His linen shirt clung so tight to his chest that it seemed a second skin, betraying his own discomfort. At last he reached for her hand, the touch barely calming her heart as she squeezed back. She could no longer discern the cry of the osprey or the incessant gentle hum of the cicada. She could hear nothing but her William as he proposed marriage to her. Instantly, the wholeness of her world spun around, colliding with all her hopes and dreams. Yes! Yes! She would be Mrs. William Blount.

He shared with her with how encroaching thoughts of her had consumed him all along his ride to Wilmington. More than anything, he wanted her near him, to be his wife, but he was first obligated to return to New Bern in Craven County, returning for her just as soon as he possibly could. He really hated to wait. She barely heard all he said, her mind full of his proposal as he listed his duties and obligations as a paymaster to the North Carolina Regiments, his business in New Bern and Martinsborough, and his commitments to his brothers. He kept returning to talk of a wedding, gifting her with a wedding ring and his oath of faithfulness.

They talked on and on, losing track of all time and all else around them, as she sat beside him, glowing as warm and bright as the setting sun. She realized it was time to return home, knowing her world had been forever changed. Being the sole girl in her family, her wedding would be exuberant. William sat bursting with pride, assuredly picking up the reins and turning the carriage toward the Grainger homestead in the shadow of dusk. Their hands entwined with each other along the cooling roadway back, their touch secure in the promises made, beginning that binding that would last their lifetime.

Upon their arrival, they approached her mother as one. William respectfully asked for Molsey's hand in marriage. Mrs. Grainger's face sparkled with delight; her heartfelt wish for her daughter's happiness would soon come true. Happily, she solidified the pending union with her blessing. The trio, united in this agreement, excitedly spoke of future wedding plans. Lists would be filled, relatives invited, and a beautiful new wedding gown reflective of the brand-new life Molsey was embarking on would be designed and created. They would post the wedding bans in a Wilmington newspaper, though not at St. James Episcopal Church since the rector had left, heralding the closing of the church.

Wedding plans would be somewhat stifled due to the distance between the couple. The war with England raged throughout the colonies; often Molsey's ears echoed with the booming of distant cannons. Travel, at best, was perilous. On the morrow, William would leave for the north section of North Carolina. They would have to depend on postal correspondence, not exactly the most reliable thing since mail was often lost or stolen. They promised to write each other as often as they could before the wedding, hoping to somehow finalize the arrangements.

The morning whispered its greetings at the rising of a flaming orange sun, announcing in its somnambulant silence the time of parting. Saying good-bye to William ached almost beyond endurance. William waved bravely from his carriage as he trotted away to New Bern, promising to return for his betrothed. Molsey tightly clutched the gleaming ring on her finger as she watched the carriage disappear over the hill's crest. The sparkling stone did nothing to ease the emptiness and longing in her heart. She had no way of knowing this heartache would become part of her life with William.

∼ell))∾

History has not recorded the courtship or marriage of William Blount to Ms. Molsey Grainger. Marriage certificates were not required in North Carolina before 1780, yet this union forever altered both of their lives and that of their families'. Molsey and William Blount were wed on February 21, 1778, most likely in her Wilmington home, at the height of the Revolutionary War. At the time of his marriage proposal, William worked in the New Bern area, the 1778 colonial capital of North Carolina. He was probably still living with his father at Blount Hall, a cotton and tobacco plantation located south of Martinsborough, North Carolina (today the city of Greenville), a two-day carriage drive from Wilmington. This distance means that the wedding most likely took place in Molsey's hometown. Prior to their marriage, it would have been inappropriate and highly unlikely that she would travel with William to his home in Pitt County, more than one hundred miles north.

Colonial society set the boundaries for an engaged couple's courtship. In the 1700s courting couples spent time together, usually in the company of others, in informal pursuits. Long walks, carriage rides, or talks on a porch helped the couple get acquainted. Presumably, William and Molsey spent such times together, yet due to the war and the great distance from each other's homes, courtship would have been difficult, and times together would have been minimal.

Questions loom about their courtship. Did they spend evenings on the porch? Did they take walks along Wilmington streets? Were they in love? Was it a marriage of convenience and economic gain for William Blount? Such questions are left unanswered in history's tomes. Perhaps future historians will be able to dig out more of the details concerning their courtship. For now, history indicates that throughout the violent time of the Revolutionary War, normal courtship and common marriage practices were disrupted.

Surprisingly, Southern attitudes regarding courtship and sexuality during those times seem ambivalent. While chaperones were the norm, and keeping a watchful eye on a couple was important, cohabitation, bundling, and premarital sex were also common in early North Carolina courtships. Richard Godbeer notes in *Sexual Revolution in Early America* (John Hopkins Press 2002), "Popular attitudes toward premarital sex were…much more permissive on both sides of the Atlantic than church or legal officials would have liked." Elite colonial families did their best to exert strong control over extramarital sexuality, though they seldom succeeded.

The practice of bundling was permitted across all Southern social classes. Based on the biblical story of Ruth and Boaz, bundling or bed courting was permissible for couples who were seriously courting. Bundling was meant to help ensure the young couple was compatible. Basically, the couple would spend the night together in bed with a few ground rules, one of them being that underclothes had to remain in place. A bundling sack was placed around the young adults, allowing the couple to communicate but not participate in any form of sex. An alternative was a bundling board, used to keep the partners separated during the night. The original purpose for making sure the couple was compatible was often ignored as the couple engaged in other forms of compatibility.

As a genteel young woman in 1777, Molsey may have developed a strict standard of behavior. It appears that Southern chivalry came into play for young ladies of affluent families. Molsey probably engaged in this sense of premarital chastity as evidenced by her politeness, intrigue, respect, and gentleness. White gentlemen played by different social rules and standards. They were free to exercise their sexuality through cohabiting, fornication, or having multiple partners without condemnation. Ultimately, history is silent on the intimacies of Molsey and William Blount.

The absence of any information concerning William and Molsey's courtship and marriage leaves historians to speculate about this intimate part of their lives. The reader is left to form their own opinions. Andrew Gardner remarks in the magazine *Colonial Williamsburg* that, "Beyond doubt, most people stayed strictly within the bounds of propriety, but in the mid to late 1700s, more than one girl in three was pregnant when she walked down the aisle." William and Molsey Blount professed their nuptials on February 21, 1778. Their first child was born and died in 1779. There is no month or day recorded anywhere for the birth.

Their marriage most likely took place at the Grainger home rather than in a church. St. James Episcopal Church, the Grainger family's traditional place of worship, had been abandoned early in the Revolutionary War because of its association with England. William Blount's family seemed uninterested in religion. This leads to the belief that they were married in her home instead of a church.

Marrying into the Blount family would have been a formidable experience for any young woman. By 1778, in the middle of the Revolutionary War, the Blount family had become powerful, influential, and wealthy members of society. To better understand the character, challenges, changes, and opportunities that awaited Molsey in her marriage, it is best to have a basic knowledge of William Blount.

Masterson, in his noted biography, *William Blount* (Louisiana State University Press 1954), portrays the Blount family of Pitt County as part of a class of businessmen and politicians that would "become to many other nations the personification of our national character." Poised at the ideal time in history to benefit from the resources and opportunities offered by this fledgling nation, William, along with his brothers John and Thomas, were able to amass their fortunes in land speculation; merchandizing; manufacturing tar, turpentine, timber, and nails; and the international shipping of materials all over the world.

Similar to the Kennedy clan of the 1960s, the Blount brothers formed a powerful, intelligent, and political—though at times questionable—trio. Jacob Blount, their father, encouraged his sons' business, political, and military interests. He had become a wealthy landowner and wanted to pass those skills and riches on to his sons. Jacob built the family plantation, Blount Hall, south of Martinsborough, North Carolina. The house was constructed on what is now Blount Hall Road, near the corner of State Road 1103, north of Grifton, North Carolina.

Blount Hall, Pitt County. William Blount lived here until he married Molsey Blount in 1778. Their son Blount was taken to Blount Hall for burial having died in October 1790. Blount Hall was still standing until it burned in 1964.

William came into the world on Easter Sunday, March 26, 1749, at Rosefield in Bertie County, the home of his maternal grandmother. Born into a life of wealth and privilege, he attended a preparatory school in New Bern, North Carolina. William developed an interest in the family mercantile business at an early age. When he turned fourteen years of age in 1763, his mother, Barbara Gray, tragically died in the spring; two days later, his older sister Barbara also died. Bereft of a mother for his seven children, Jacob soon remarried. Stability returned to Blount Hall until Jacob's second wife also died. Her death left two more children to be raised by yet a second stepmother, Jacob's third wife.

Though history does not reveal when William first met Molsey Grainger, he most likely was in his late teens or early twenties. He began training in his teens to manage the family mercantile interests along the Pamlico River. Learning his father's business required him as the oldest son to travel throughout the Cape Fear area, near the town of Wilmington. He also developed an interest in land speculation since Jacob encouraged his sons to invest in land. As a young adult, William became interested in investing in western lands. He believed that the future of his newly developing nation was on the other side of the Appalachian Mountains, eventually becoming obsessed with land speculation.

During the Revolutionary War in 1778, William and his father served as paymasters to the North Carolina militia, roaming throughout the state. William accepted the appointment as regimental paymaster in the New Bern district for the Third North Carolina Regiment. He did not actually fight on a battlefield, though he joined the regiment's northern march in defense of Philadelphia against General Howe's royal forces.

His work in recruiting and equipping Patriot forces continued for the next three years. As providers of supplies to the military, William and his family aligned themselves with the Patriot cause, profiting financially and politically from the war. Serving as a paymaster opened up ample opportunities for future political positions. William met George Washington in Philadelphia in 1777. Impressed with the young Blount, Washington became a constant and stable political force in William's life. Washington was so impressed by the young William at this meeting that it would influence his future selection of governor for the Territory southwest of the Ohio River.

In the midst of a raging continental war, William somehow managed to court and wed the lovely Molsey Grainger. The one hundred miles between the couple's homes did nothing to deter him. The age difference was also ignored. They married a month before his thirtieth birthday; she was barely seventeen years old. Why would these two people decide to marry when America's future seemed so uncertain? Historians record a handful of clues as to how they met but no definitive answer as to why they married.

The Graingers and the Blounts shared several personal acquaintances, business relationships, and political ties, all of which favored the couple's meeting each other. Before the war, William traveled extensively throughout eastern North Carolina and to the Wilmington area, seeking investors and buyers for his family's mercantile and agricultural businesses and speculating on land. At the same time, Molsey's father, Caleb, was conducting business with merchants throughout eastern North Carolina. William was sixteen when Caleb died in 1765 and was involved in his father's shipping ties to Wilmington, North Carolina, an important seaport in the mid-1700s. It was entirely possible that Caleb Grainger and Jacob Blount knew each other prior to Molsey's birth.

The Revolutionary War was another common factor between the two families. As William traveled through North Carolina as paymaster during the Revolutionary War, he probably met up with Molsey's brothers or other relatives who were serving in the militia. Two of William's own brothers also served during the war, increasing the possibility the families would meet. At such a gathering, William could have spied his future bride, eyeing her from a distance. As she grew into the dark beauty mentioned later in their shared history, more intentional visits to Wilmington seemed likely.

If it was not the business and military connections the two families shared that brought them together, it was the political connections. Both families were closely connected to statesmen Cornelius Harnett and Richard Caswell of North Carolina. Caleb had even named a child after Cornelius, Molsey's older brother. Cornelius Harnett was a well-respected Patriot. He owned a plantation next to Caleb Grainger when Molsey was a small child. Harnett and Grainger had been Masonic brothers in Wilmington. The Blounts, Graingers, and Harnetts shared the same political views concerning British dominance in the colony. William could have easily met Molsey through any of these relationships.

Richard Caswell, who eventually became the first and fifth governor of the Tar Heel state, might well have played a role as matchmaker as well. Caswell had been a surveyor, lawyer, and a member of the Colonial Assembly in 1754, just as Molsey's father, Caleb Grainger, had been in 1747. Caswell served as Major

General at the Battle of Alamance in 1771, a battle that William's father, Jacob, reportedly also fought in. Caswell was deeply involved in Revolutionary War politics, impacting Molsey's brothers—Cornelius, Caleb, and John—all of whom were soldiers in the fight for freedom.

Lastly, both families all knew Richard Blackledge and his sons. Both the Graingers and Blounts were interested in the politics and business finesse of the Blackledge family. William and Molsey would even name one of their sons Richard Blackledge Blount.

The marriage of William and Molsey Blount created an important business and political alliance, a common practice in colonial America. For William, his marriage to Molsey provided for a future of further wealth and privilege. For Molsey, her marriage provided her with security and someone to care for her. Through marriage, William inherited all his wife's lands and belongings. In *Marriage in Colonial North Carolina*, Maren Wood reminds us that a wedding was more than just a wedding between the young couple. This arrangement was a "commitment between two families that tied them together socially, financially, and politically." The groom's family would have wanted their son to marry a respectable woman, someone who would bring money into the family, someone like Molsey Grainger. Mrs. Grainger would have wished to see her daughter well cared for throughout her life.

Caleb Grainger's *Last Will and Testament* (1765) provided Molsey with land, furniture, slaves, and personal possessions. According to his will, Molsey inherited:

> two Negro Wenches and what Children they now have, the names of the Wenches is, Little Hager and Venice...in case either of said Wenches should die before my said daughter comes to the Age of Seventeen or day of Marriage, that then, and in such Case my Executors shall replace such Negro or Negroes out of My General Stock of Negroes to be a Breeding Wench or Wenches." She also inherited one "lott of Land in

Wilmington, Containing Thirty feet front upon the Street, and the Common Depth of Lotts which I have sold upon said Street.

Since it was unclear in the will where this property was specifically located, her father's vague reference allowed the executors to survey any lot formerly owned by Caleb for Molsey. Her father's will also added to her marriage dowry:

one Good Bed & Furniture, two Mahogany Tables, Six Mahogany Chairs, one Large Mahogany framed Looking Glass, and Such of my Plate as I shall leave a list Inclosed in my will; all which things as aforesaid shall be delivered to her at the Age of Seventeen Years, or day of Marriage.

Caleb's direction for disbursement of these items coincides with William's proposal and Molsey's age.

As this seventeen-year-old war bride left with William to their new home, along with the slaves and furniture, she packed the remaining items left to her by her father. As noted in her father's last will and testament, Molsey was the recipient of a complete dinnerware service:

1 Doz Table Knives & forks, Silver Handles, 1 doz Desart Ditto Silver handles, 1 Silver Butter Boat, 1 Do. Tea pott, 1 Ditto Milk Pot, 1 Dx Silver Salts & Shovels, 1 Silver Salver, 1 Set of Casters with Silver Tongs, 1 Soup Spoon, silver, Half a Doxen Silver Table Spoons, Tea Spoons.

There is one last note before leaving Caleb's will. An interesting phrase is included toward the end of this document regarding his longtime friend Cornelius Harnett. Caleb makes a request; he directs, "...my Dear and ever Worthy Friend Mr. Corn. Harnett have purchased out of my Estate a neat Mourning Ring which I begg he may wear in remembrance of his Sincair Friend & Brother." Mourning rings were popular, a keepsake of a deceased loved one. The ring would have contained a small cutting of the deceased person's hair within the design. The designing and wearing of mourning rings was well-known among the Graingers. Twenty years later, Molsey's children also made mourning rings following family deaths.

After their wedding in late February, the couple left Molsey's mother and brothers behind and headed north to their new home. Their personal carriage, along with an entourage of several loaded wagons, would usher the couple into the North Carolina capital, New Bern. William had spent time before the wedding in finding a comfortable home for them. Based in New Bern as paymaster for the militia, he had ample time to choose their new house, ensuring his ability to stay close to political opportunities. The new home, close to Blount Hall, was also near his brother's homes and businesses in Washington and Martinsborough, North Carolina.

Today only one Blount home survives in North Carolina. The restored home in Tarborough, North Carolina, belonged to William's brother Thomas Blount. William's birth home, Blount Hall, burned down in the 1960s. The numerous homes William or Molsey owned are all gone. For Molsey Blount, loss and displacement became a hallmark of her life. She lost the homeland she knew from birth, all her homes, friends, and even her first child.

5

Sometime in 1779—
New Bern, North Carolina

His name was Cornelius—her first baby, her sweet baby boy. His silken infant hair smelled like sunshine on lilies. His tiny fingers had curled around her one finger like vines around a trellis. His cornflower blue eyes had glimmered innocently, along with his soft mewling. Her firstborn, her sweet little Cornelius, lay so cold and still, and her arms felt so bereft. She traced each small facet of his face, so like his father's. His mouth was the delicate shape of his mother's. Cradling him close, her heart broke in pieces, and her soul withered. The hot, searing, prickly pain clamped on to her stomach and flowed over into her guts. She grasped at her last shred of dignity, then wailed, her scream outdistanced only by the dark. The baby's limp body followed her to the floor, entwined in her arms, lifeless, a cold little rag doll. Her emotions ran a gauntlet of pain and hate and anger and confusion, her mind a swirling maelstrom, sucking her into bottomless darkness and desolation. She lay on the floor, rocking her little Cornelius in some ancient rhythm of a mother's consolation to her infant. She rocked and rocked in the void, not crying or cooing. She held on to her silence, to his leaving, vaguely aware of sanity and life.

William was nowhere to be found, his habitual absence excused and understood; he was unaware, for now, of the death of his little boy. Too soon, he would return to learn of the tragic loss of his firstborn son. Little Corn, he had called him. But Hagar was here, her ever-faithful slave— no, closer than a slave, someone who had known her for as long as she could remember. Hagar, the midwife who had delivered her son to her, now attended her as comforter and counselor. She had travailed with all her might to save the boy, to no avail. Nothing she had tried had kept the wee one from slipping into eternity. Warm baths, poultices, syrups of mother's milk and herbs—nothing had worked. His little heart just couldn't go on beating. He had suddenly and frighteningly turned blue, gone before a doctor could be summoned.

Hagar knew better than to try and pick up her mistress. She knew not to take the baby away, at least not yet. Hagar lowered herself to the floor nearby, her own tears streaking down the darkness of her face. She didn't know who she was crying for—for Mistress Molsey, the baby, or herself. Her heart mourned, watching her young mistress's initiation into that part of life that brings such inexorable pain, the harsh world of death, loss, pain, and grief. The carefree, sunny days of a newlywed bride, the airiness and excitement of moving into a fresh, new home, the instantaneous joy and love that fairly burst the heart of a new mother—all had fled into the ebony pit of grief and loss. Molsey's new motherly heart had been cheated, robbed. Hagar knew all too well these losses, these pains; as a slave she had known the anguish and ongoing loss of children and husbands, the humiliation of life as a slave and the finality of death. These things had stalked her since her childhood.

Now the death angel had stalked this child, seizing his breath and silencing his heartbeat. Hagar reached for Molsey's hand, proffering comfort and care, only to be met with the young mother's back-and-forth rocking, which seemed to voicelessly repeat, "Go away! Go away!"

Venice, the other domestic slave, dared to enter the room. She studied Hagar's face, searching for a sign or some word telling her what to do. Hagar shook her head, vainly hoping Venice would understand that all was lost.

"Go git Masta Blount! Y'all git. Go!" Hagar finally shouted over the moaning of her mistress. As Molsey rocked on the cold hard floor, Hagar's world was rocked by this new injustice, another searing pain of outrage, something she couldn't control any more than the other injustices of her life.

Venice fled the house. Finding Master Blount would not be easy. He could be with any number of merchants or neighbors, perhaps at the paymaster's Office. Where should she look first? Aware that a slave running through the streets of New Bern could panic the white residents, she slowed her pace and her racing thoughts. Where could he be?

Standing quietly in the doorway of the blacksmith shop, Venice peered into the darkness. Her heart raced, and she twisted her apron strings while she dug her toes nervously into the dirt. She called out to the sweaty bulk of a man, asking if he had seen Master Blount and listening to his deep resonant voice as he replied, "He's ore dat place 'cross da street!"

Turning on her heel, she hastened to the lawyer's office. She knocked on the door with the insistence of a drummer boy, shifting on her feet, waiting for the door to open. Finally, Master Blount was at the door.

Stumbling over her words, she told him to hurry. Disbelief and confusion stumbled over his thoughts as he tried to understand what had happened at home. Venice spoke of the baby, about Molsey. "Oh, Masta, it be hor'ble!"

Shoving past the girl, William Blount's thoughts overshadowed his gentility as he awkwardly tried to outrun the fear that boiled up within. Panic twisted around his heart, apprehension consuming his breath as he neared his home. "Oh law! What has happened to my sweet Molly?" he whispered as he mounted the stairs.

Heart pounding, he found his wife on the floor, clutching his son—their child—to her breast. He bent over her, fighting to comprehend the sobs, the moans, and the tears. Gently, he sat down next to her and Hagar. Hagar looked at her master, shook her head, and silently mouthed something about the baby. He wanted to get Molsey up off the floor. Gesturing for Hagar to help, they slowly lifted the distraught mother to her feet. William wrapped his arms around his wife and baby, tears stinging his eyes as he blinked them back so no one would see. Realizing that his child was dead, he attempted to loosen his wife's grip on the cold body. Laboring to keep the child safe, to hold her angel forever, Molsey was hard-pressed to let go, continuing to stroke the body as it was taken away.

The death of her baby, the unrelenting grief, and the stark realization of life's cruelties stalked her for days, for months. Her grief had a life of its own, haunting her, visiting her in the middle of the night while dining with her husband, or while at the market. Little did she know that death waited for her again, waited to take another of her children in years to come. She would never get used to it.

✺✺✺

William and Molsey's firstborn son, Cornelius, died sometime in 1779. No record remains of the month or day of that event, just as there is no day or month in the records of his birth. In fact, little information has survived regarding his life and death. Apparently, the Blounts, or at least the historians, reconciled his death to the culture of dying in those colonial times. In those times, parents were encouraged not to get too attached to their infants since infant mortality was high—extremely high. Babies often died soon after birth from complications unknown to the medical profession. Therefore, nothing is known about the sudden, unexpected death of the Blounts' firstborn, Cornelius. History doesn't reveal where he was buried either. It's assumed he was buried in the New Bern area.

Other facts can be conjectured surrounding Cornelius Blount's birth. His birth has been simply stated having occurred in 1779, most likely around January or February. Her next child, Nancy, was born in January 1780, possibly within ten to twelve months of her son's death. Apparently, Molsey became pregnant soon after her wedding, with barely enough time to adjust to a husband, a new home, a new town, and then a pregnancy. Childbirth in colonial America was extremely difficult and dangerous from the lack of knowledge and care in regard to any complications that might arise. A colonial mother's chance of dying in childbirth was one in eight. Pregnancy was often looked upon with dread.

Experience as well as superstitions fueled the anxieties connected with childbirth. Expectant mothers were taught not to look upon a "horrible spectre" and to avoid being startled by a loud noise. If a hare ran across the path of a pregnant woman, it would cause the child to be born with a harelip, and if the mother-to-be gazed too long at the moon, it could cause the child to be a lunatic or sleepwalker. Pregnant women were encouraged to do hard manual labor, believing that would make their delivery easier.

Since doctors were not usually called to assist at birth, experienced women known as midwives assisted in the labor and delivery of children for centuries. In time, male midwives infiltrated the profession. Medical doctors did not become part of midwifery until the later part of the eighteenth century. The use of male doctors in the delivery of a difficult birth reinforced the belief that childbirth was dangerous.

The upper classes hired doctors to deliver their babies because of their success with forceps and drugs, which could ease delivery and pain. However, forceps did not ensure a healthy delivery because of the lack of sanitation and knowledge of the transmission of diseases. Until then, no painkillers were used, other than alcohol or possibly willow bark tea. The article "Childbirth in America" (University of Houston Digital Library) tells us, "Pain in childbirth was considered God's punishment for Eve's sin of eating the forbidden fruit in the Garden of Eden." Any suffering or pain was to be endured, the mother being encouraged to be patient and pray.

By the time Molsey had her first child, some new practices had been introduced. The idea of giving birth in a brightly lit room, rather than in a dark enclosed room, such as had been preferred in the early 1700s, was being practiced among the upper classes. Birthing chairs were being utilized by genteel ladies. These chairs slowly became more specialized, with handholds and set at increased height for the attendants' comfort. Husbands were encouraged to attend a birth, and even siblings were allowed to watch. Breastfeeding was popular, and most women spent a month in bed after giving birth. Molsey's slaves—in particular, Hagar—would have cared for her and Cornelius after his birth.

It has been suggested that Hagar was the midwife to Molsey at her first birth. Hagar had been owned by the Graingers prior to her move to Wilmington with the Blounts. As a slave, she had cared for Mrs. Grainger, possibly through the births of Molsey and her siblings. As a faithful household slave, Hagar's experience would have been invaluable during childbirth or a lying-in period for Molsey. She had served as slave to the Blounts for decades.

An antique birthing chair. Often affluent women used these chairs for the ease of giving birth. Popular in the eighteenth century, Molsey most likely used one during the birth of one of her nine children.

Molsey was eighteen years old when her firstborn died. Having moved away from her family, she was left with her slaves or possibly a friend for comfort throughout her grief. She had several sisters-in-law living a long carriage ride away; hopefully they provided her with some comfort too. The female relatives were Martha Baker Blount, referred to as Sukey, the first wife of Thomas Blount, living in Tarborough, and Mary Blount, wife of John Gray Blount and affectionately called Sister Polly, who lived in Washington, North Carolina.

William would not have been able to remain by her side every day. He was too busy in the business of the Revolutionary War. As paymaster to colonial troops, he had the job of disbursing their salaries, paying the accounts of the militia, and purchasing supplies for Craven County. He was deeply embroiled in the reorganization of battalions and supplying them for their march to South Carolina in defense of Charleston.

Thomas, John, and William Blount, due to their positions as merchants and military men, rode the crest of financial success. They bought tar, pitch, lumber, staves, shingles, and tobacco from the locals, along with salt, cloth, shoes, and weapons needed by the militia. William was shrewdly prospering during the war and starting out in the initial stages of establishing his career while others were losing their lives. He became a trustee of the newly formed New Bern Academy, a public school for boys of the town. It wasn't long before he became General Horatio Gates's official commissary. His too-familiar absences from his family were becoming the norm.

Yet he was not totally unavailable to Molsey. By March 1779, she was once more pregnant. Having another baby the next year helped assuage her grief. On average, most women had nine children, typically born two years apart due to breastfeeding, a natural way of spacing children. Conversely, wealthier women who did not nurse their babies had more children utilizing wet nurses instead. With slaves and domestic help to do the chores, Molsey could easily have considered another child within a few months of the death of her son.

Braving another pregnancy with the fear of a miscarriage and possibly dying in childbirth, Molsey bore her second child in January of 1780, a girl named Ann Blount, possibly after William's younger sister Ann. History, however, would call her by another name. Nancy is a derivative of the name Ann, a common name during colonial times. Thus, her name would be Nancy, as agreed upon by William and Molsey. William obviously delighted in using nicknames. As noted, he referred to his wife as Molsey, though calling her Molly during their early married years.

Motherhood did not escape Molsey this time. In fact, she was consumed with her new child, perhaps because she was hounded by the knowledge that Nancy could die at any time from disease or complications. Though William remained constrained by war and business, Molsey began to enjoy being a mother. The month Nancy was born, William began a ten-year term as the representative to North Carolina's General Assembly. Since the assembly met in New Bern, William would have been close by for the birth, possibly sharing Molsey's concerns. Yet his political interests would soon call him to the Assembly Chamber. For Molsey, motherhood took up all her time. Counting baby fingers and toes would have been more important than a veto or a vote.

At a time of changing gender roles for the Blounts, the question of how much input William had in the raising of his children arises. If we assume that his model of the family rested on patriarchy, with his expected role as that of the main authority and wage earner in the family, we might also assume that he was aware of Molsey's need of support and companionship during this time. However, history holds that William preferred to be a part of the political, military, and business machine of New Bern and subsequently was often away from home. This would have left his wife with a larger portion of the household responsibilities and child rearing. Therefore, it easy to see how Molsey, upon the birth of her second child, took upon herself a more independent role as woman, wife, and mother. As a result of this, she would have gained greater status and functioned in a wider range of roles within her community and family. Her and William's marriage reflects the thoughts of historian Steven Mintz in *Mothers and*

Fathers in America: Looking Backward, Looking Forward: "blended together an odd mixture of patriarchy and wifely independence."

As William made plans to switch over from representing New Bern in local political circles to representing New Bern in state affairs, a change occurred in his home. Molsey's mother, Mary Grainger, came to visit them—a seemingly extended visit. Mrs. Grainger probably came to New Bern to assist with the birth and care of Nancy. Colonial childbirth was often attended by older and more experienced women.

Another reason for Molsey's mother to be within the Blount household was to provide her with more safety during the war. Her presence in the Blount's home was meant to be temporary. As she and her daughter came together, it made them realize their need for each other. As a widow, Mary Grainger had been living in Wilmington with her son John and the slaves. Her other sons had left home to serve in the war efforts. It is doubtful she would have left John alone in Wilmington for too long, thus the basis for a temporary visit. When Wilmington became a haven for British forces toward the war's end, Mary returned to Wilmington to settle her affairs before returning to the Blounts.

Mary Grainger had sold Masonborough and Sans Souci by 1780 or 1781. She still held property in Wilmington, real estate that would later be part of a lawsuit against her. She had numerous slaves to sell and monies from her husband's estate to distribute to her sons. Though the exact year she moved in with the Blounts isn't known, when she did permanently move in with them, she had her own resources. Even so, she willingly made herself dependent upon her son-in-law's authority. He would manage her affairs for over ten years.

Though the ambitious William was absorbed in his political functions within the General Assembly and as the representative in the House of Commons, he decided to leave New Bern, moving his family to a new plantation, Piney Grove. This one-thousand-acre plantation on the Great Contentnea Creek in Dobbs County became a hub of activity for the Blount family. What was once

Dobbs County is now a part of Greene and Lenoir Counties. The exact location of Piney Grove has been lost through the years. William and Molsey were now closer to his family. Blount Hall and his father were about ten miles to the east. John Gray and Thomas, his brothers, were also closer. The close proximity of these homes initiated a more diverse and accessible business and family arrangement. The geographic location of the three homes created excellent water resources along the Tar River. Editor Alice Keith in volume 3 of the *John Gray Blount Papers* (Christian Printing Company 1959) states that these locations provided ideal transportation by land transportation in a way that allowed for the brothers to continue in their speculations of "land values, commodities, debts, money issues, and new property transfers in which to gamble."

All three volumes of *The John Gray Blount Papers* provide an exceptional source of information, tracing the Blounts' movements from 1764 to 1802. William's movement from New Bern to the Piney Grove Plantation reveals that by 1781 or 1782, the family was living within fifteen miles of his father. Molsey, with the help of slaves and domestic servants, began the arduous work of refurnishing and decorating a large home. Nancy was one year old at the time and still the delight of Molsey's heart. Her husband's interest in the diversity of his business interests led him to build sawmills and granaries and possibly a distillery on the property. Production of tar, turpentine, tobacco, and corn supported the Blount brothers' legacy for decades.

Molsey became a more intimate part of the Blount clan. Together, the Blount brothers and their wives attended the theater, dances, and family gatherings. Now that William's family was within a day's carriage ride, more celebrations and get-togethers were planned. Prosperity, as the war began to come to an end, embraced this family like a ship's sail embraces the wind.

By 1781, Cornwallis surrendered in Yorktown, Virginia, to General George Washington. Though skirmishes and battles clattered throughout valleys and towns, Britain had given up its authority over the colonies. The sovereignty of the United States had been won, with the final Treaty of Paris making independence complete. By January 27, 1781, William was a part of that independence. He traveled north to Halifax, North Carolina, to take his seat in the third session of the state's House of Representatives. Thus, he continued a series of never-ending travels away from Molsey.

Most likely Molsey grew to resent his frequent trips away from her, at least in the beginning, but she had to adjust. Colonial politicians were often away from their families. His constant and predictable absences must not be judged too harshly as uncaring for his family by twenty-first-century American standards. Colonial culture dictated that affluent political men had to be fully dedicated to their career, which meant constantly traveling to get ahead. Just as William was fully invested in his political future, Molsey was as fully dedicated to her family, finding herself pregnant yet again.

6

April 1782—
Piney Grove, North Carolina

The growing ache in Molsey's back alarmed her. She knew what it meant, yet her mind filled with dread at what it forewarned. She wasn't at all ready. The months of discomfort, swollen feet, restless nights, and food cravings would soon be over. But where was William? She imagined him far away, busy with something that had nothing to do with her, nothing to do with the family, and just plain nothing to do with anything important. She strained laboriously to her feet, leaning heavily on the arm of the chair, moaning with the rhythm of the throbbing, rising pain. Repositioning her feet, she gave up trying to straighten her skirt, preferring to arch her back as the palms of her hands braced her hips.

Slowly and deliberately, she ambled, heavy with child, toward the front door. She hoped to find her mother rocking on the porch. Bracing herself against the door, she called to her mother, but no one answered. Suddenly, a gush of warm water flooded down her leg, circling in a pool about her feet. Aghast at the indignity of soiled small garments she turned, aware of this new urgency of the pending birth, looking for someone—anyone to help her.

Sall, racing from the kitchen at the sound of her mistress's calls, rushed to her side. Wrapping her arms about Molsey's thickened girth, she guided her toward the stairway. Hollering for Hagar or Venice or anyone, Sall supported Molsey for the long struggle up the stairs to her bedchamber. Molsey's mother appeared amidst all the commotion of her daughter's moans and the hollering. Mrs. Grainger, seeing her daughter aided up the stairs, hastened in relief past the lumbering couple, intent on arriving at the bedchamber before her daughter and the slave. She snatched the linen curtains, closing them against the mounting fear and anxiety.

As Molsey awkwardly climbed onto the four-poster bed, the women sighed with relief, only to hear her moans and cries escalate. She arched her back, slowly rolling side to side, unable to get comfortable. She needed to be on the birthing chair, not the bed. The unborn child was releasing its claim on her body, demanding attention and insisting on passage into the world. Hagar entered the room, and now the stage was set for the birth. Hagar had helped deliver her other two children and could be trusted with birthing this baby too. Carefully, the women aided Molsey, easing her over to the birthing chair.

Meanwhile, Molsey's other child, Nancy, came peering around the corner, curious with all the fuss and commotion. Just two years old, she was a lot like her inquisitive father and occasionally shy mother. But she sure wasn't shy now; little Nancy tottered into the bedchamber, her scrunched-up determined expression daring anyone to stop her from reaching her mother. Mrs. Grainger hastened to intercept her granddaughter, believing her presence would upset Molsey. Her gentle grandmotherly arms scooped Nancy up as another cry came from Molsey. Nancy would just have to wait outside the room with her Mammy Venice. Later, her mother's reassuring hugs would console Nancy. For now, the toddler reluctantly trailed along with Venice, her small hand grasped snugly as they made their way down the hall.

In this ancient ritual of birth pangs and fitful moments of rest, Molsey gasped and strained. She eagerly participated in the demanding act of pushing life from her body. The birthing chair creaked and heaved with each contraction. Hagar sat firmly on a stool between Molsey's legs, focused on catching the baby as it emerged. Mrs. Grainger held her daughter's hand, patting and stroking the soft fingers and arm. The sole desire to be loosed

72

from the grip of the relentless stabbing pains moved Molsey steadily through the hours of intense laboring.

A warm, sweaty, pungent odor permeated the bedchamber as the child slipped from its mother. Finally, bathed in exhaustion and relief, Molsey collapsed in the chair, her baby born. The wee form emerged covered in blood and shiny birth fluids—another little girl. At the first glance of the naked newborn, Hagar smiled broadly, cradling the baby in her big hands. Wiping the infant with a towel and cleaning out her mouth called forth the most anticipated wail of the newest Blount. The baby's cry soon turned to cooing, and Molsey breathed a sigh of relief. It seemed that this little one was healthy. For now, her baby only showed the signs of a normal birth and delivery. With a scrunched-up nose and wrinkly face, this sweet one was already blinking at the world, kicking her feet, and calling out for attention.

William's attention had been focused most recently on political matters in North Carolina. Molsey dearly felt her husband's absences. His travels were the one hardship in her marriage that was so difficult to bear. His travels serenaded him about what he seemed to love most—politics and land—away from Molsey's core need for his companionship and help. She longed for his stories about Richard Caswell or Abner Nash. And now she especially needed him, but he had stayed away, immersed in the politics of Hillsborough or New Bern while his daughter was being birthed. Another distant memory flashed through her longing. His trip to Halifax back in January had stolen him away when she most needed him to help in the decisions concerning new slaves and the tobacco field.

As Molsey contemplated her husband's absences, her thoughts were pulled back to the newest member of the Blount family. This little dark-haired baby needed a name, and her father wasn't here to help in the decision. Molsey wondered if the little one would learn to be as patient as she was when it came to her father.

Who knew how long he would be gone? As days and weeks passed, Molsey found herself calling the baby sweetie and my little one. Her mother began to insist that Molsey settle on a more appropriate name for the little girl, so in honor of her mother, her sister-in-law, and, secretly, herself, she announced the child would be called Mary Louisa.

Washed in contentment whenever she cradled her sweet little baby girl in her arms, Molsey snuggled the babe close to her heart. Each and every time, little Mary Louisa would root around for her mother's breast. With each feeding, the love of her baby consumed Molsey. The babe instinctively delighted in the warm nuzzling that resulted from her search for more milk. When Mary Louisa finally dropped off to sleep in her mother's arms that day, Molsey lingered over her daughter's perfect tiny fingers and soft cheek. She pondered her child's future. Would she marry too? Would she want to be a mother? Would she miss her husband? Like most parents, Molsey only saw goodness and greatness in her child's life. Little did Molsey know, her little girl would grow up missing both her parents, even as Molsey now missed her William.

~ꝛꝛꝛꝛ~

Molsey's third baby, Mary Louisa, was born at Piney Grove. The annals of history give not a hint as to whether William was actually present at her birth or naming, or even if he was present at any of his children's births. The historical record simply states that Molsey gave birth to her third child sometime in 1782. Named Mary Louisa, she would be called Louisa throughout her whole life. That fit in well with the Blount family custom of preferring nicknames and middle names for everyday use. William, after all, had been called Billy by his brothers while growing up. He had no middle name. His daughter Ann was Nancy, his brother Thomas was Tom on occasion, and other relatives were given a host of nicknames.

During the last part of the eighteenth century, it became common for wives in affluent families to address their husband by the formal title of *mister*. Whether or not Molsey called her husband Mr. Blount is not clear. Since the Blounts were known for their aristocratic propriety, there is a possibility that she would have called him by his formal name, at least in public.

Another formal and popular rite of passage in colonial times that the Blounts may have indulged in involved the tradition of formally baptizing or christening a child. Though not a particularly religious couple, the Blounts maintained an outward connection with a church. Therefore, it is entirely plausible that the Blounts adhered to this naming ceremony or social presentation ritual in order to maintain their sense of propriety and tradition. Molsey was a former member of the local Episcopal Church. William had maintained the family's connection to this denomination in their move to New Bern. Whether Nancy and Louisa were actually christened has not been firmly established.

The Blount daughters were born two years apart and remained close to each other throughout most their lives. All the Blount children, when living home with Molsey and William, remained close to their maternal grandmother, who also lived with them on the plantation. Mrs. Grainger helped in overseeing their upbringing. She became their constant source of care, particularly in the absence of their parents.

But in 1783 something strange happened, something that raises a question for the twenty-first-century reader. No reason seems to assuage one's discomfort concerning what went on. In a letter dated July 18, 1783, from Thomas Blount to John Gray Blount, he mentioned that little Nancy, who was staying at Blount Hall with family, "has had three violent fits of the ague & fever." Why was Molsey and William's three-year-old child living at Blount Hall, over ten miles from her birth home? At first sight, it would appear that little Nancy was temporarily visiting Blount Hall and became ill. However, that reasoning does not hold up under historical scrutiny. The fact is that throughout her young life and into her adulthood, Nancy lived with her Uncle Thomas and Aunt Ann. She never returned to live with her parents in North Carolina.

Repeated references in the *John Gray Blount Papers* refer to the fact that Nancy lived with Thomas in Tarborough, his estate on the Tar River. Complicating this information are other references to the second daughter, Louisa. She apparently also went to live with her sister Nancy at Uncle Thomas's estate. However, unlike Nancy, Louisa occasionally returned to Piney Grove and her parents. What could have happened in Molsey and William's life that would have led to their three-year-old daughter living elsewhere? After the loss of their firstborn to death and with their third child only one year old, why did they leave young Nancy with relatives? There are few available clues to those questions.

It is possible that Nancy, as a toddler, was visiting Blount Hall with Molsey. Seeing how sweet the little girl was, her paternal grandfather and stepmother may have asked if she could stay for a while. While there, the child became critically ill with yellow fever, scarlet fever, or malaria, leading Thomas to mention her in a letter to his brother John. This theory may help one understand how this dilemma may have begun, but it does nothing to explain Nancy's permanent arrangement in living away from her parents.

Another theory may be connected with Thomas's first wife's death. In March 1783, his wife, Mary Baker Blount, died and his infant son followed her in death just a few days later. The exact cause of these deaths has been lost to history, but one can well imagine how alone and desperately depressed Thomas might have been feeling. His sister Ann, also a widow, moved in with Thomas in Tarborough to help care for him. Somewhere during that time, Nancy, and later Louisa, arrived, staying until they were young adults.

Without a clear understanding as to why Molsey's two daughters do not live with her, it can be easy to judge the situation too harshly, thinking the parents were unable or unwilling to care for their children. Thinking the best, it is hoped that Molsey and William agreed to this arrangement due to some benefit for their children. Perhaps the young Nancy was left with William's brother while Molsey recovered from an illness or depression or an accident, and the young girl became very attached to her uncle and aunt. Unfortunately that argument isn't very strong when one remembers that Molsey's mother lived with her and, with the help of loving and doting slaves, would have cared for the children if Molsey fell ill. Whatever the reason behind her two daughters living apart from her, it has been lost in the annals of time.

The ever-present knowledge that their children could also be lost to them through diseases and illnesses was a disquieting fact for colonial mothers. The prospect of living until their first birthday was not a guaranteed possibility for young children. Nearly 30–40 percent of children did not live long enough to see their first birthday. The causes behind this high rate of infant mortality were varied. Plantations and cities of colonial North Carolina were not known for hygienically healthy conditions. Unaware of the potential dangers caused by poor sanitation and polluted drinking water, children were at high risk of death. People were knowledgeable about a multitude of contagious diseases but not how these diseases passed on to people. Children regularly died from diphtheria, the ubiquitous malaria fever, deadly yellow and scarlet fever, influenza, measles, mumps, and whooping cough, suffering in the arms of their helpless parents due to the unavailability of successful medical treatment.

Poor health conditions thrived in the warm, moist climate. Since North Carolina contained important seaport destinations for pirates, Caribbean privateers, and slave ships, diseases arrived part and parcel with the ships' cargoes, creeping stealthily across the land. Mosquitoes carried malaria or yellow fever, spreading like wildfire due to poorly drained rivers, standing water, and swampy regions. Eventually coastal ports that took in ships from Africa and the Caribbean quarantined these vessels, but by then these diseases were already rampantly spreading throughout the South.

These highly contagious diseases easily spread in port cities and urban areas. Travelers and slaves arriving in Wilmington or New Bern or Jacksonville brought other illnesses with them— tuberculosis, plague, smallpox, hookworms, typhoid, and dysentery. There were no cures for these deadly diseases in the late 1780s.

As mentioned in Thomas Blount's letter, three-year-old Nancy was recovering from "fits of the ague & fever." Most likely, a mosquito had bitten her, transmitting yellow fever to the little girl. Usually transmitted by mosquitoes, the illness would begin with a headache, followed with a high fever, then a yellowing of the victim's skin within a few days, indicating a problem with the liver. Epidemics of yellow fever occurred all the time throughout the colonial period in North Carolina. Most residents moved away from an outbreak or isolated themselves in their homes. Little Nancy suffered violent fits when fevered, news that would cause any parent to pray for the child's life. Nancy survived these fits, but yellow fever would continue to plague the Blount family throughout Molsey's life.

Throughout the Blount family history, malaria was another common affliction. Malaria is transmitted by a deadly mosquito. William was often laid low by this recurring disease. Many Carolina plantations grew rice, a favorite environment for the malaria parasite that lives inside the mosquito. With an abundance of slaves working the rice fields, the disease rapidly spread throughout the colony.

Freedom also spread throughout the land after the Revolutionary War, rapidly taking root in the new state of North Carolina. Cornwallis had surrendered to George Washington in 1781, but the war didn't officially end until 1783. The battered towns and cities were soon reconstructed and became bustling communities again, and William Blount secured his position as part of that change.

As William Blount's political career sprouted, it appeared that his marriage to Molsey was changing. Their marriage became more defined by his frequent travels to political meetings, debates, and elections than by family concerns. Also, a lot of his time was taken up with a plethora of business transactions and land deals. After the Revolutionary War, the new American government decided to sell the confiscated lands left behind by Loyalists who had fled back to England. The Blount brothers were among those eager to purchase these lands. William became involved in the buying and selling of huge amounts of land for a quick sale and a quick profit.

William left for Philadelphia in April of 1782, not returning to Piney Grove until almost a year later, in March of 1783. Upon his return, he realized that his home state was in dire financial straits, virtually on the brink of ruin. He continued to attend the General Assembly, making frequent trips to New Bern or Halifax, leaving his wife and family alone for days at a time. While Nancy was at her paternal grandparents' home, critically ill in July of 1783, Molsey was at home with one-year-old Louisa, pregnant again.

The year 1783 seems pivotal for the Blounts. William's frequent journeys left him relating to his brothers just how much he missed his family. He was determined to better balance his career with his family obligations. History raises the question as to whether or not Blount was ever able to achieve this goal—a debatable subject. After his long absence from the family, William admitted he was comfortable at home, and even grumbled when his obligations called him away yet again. The couple both wanted more intimacy and time together. They somehow managed to attend plays, dances, and horse races and make several visits with his family. Molsey particularly loved the carriage rides and time with her horses.

William's letters hinted of her interest in sharing his political journeys and land speculation adventures, or maybe her motivation to go along with him was founded on her reluctance to be left behind. Balancing the role of travel companion to her husband and being a mother would not be easy for her. Soon, another pregnancy would confine her to home.

William writes something interesting in a letter to a business friend, hinting at his relationship with Molsey. It seems that he hasn't been completely honest with her, withholding information from her. In September of 1783, for the first time in the *John Gray*

Blount Papers, William's comments to a business colleague seem a bit mysterious. In his discussion concerning a debt of 640 pounds he was handling for Mrs. Grainger, he asked that his colleague and friend Richard Dobbs Spaight keep the information about the transaction hidden from Molsey because if she knew, "it will be subject to misrepresentation & misconstruction." This suggests that William was working to protect Molsey from the complexities of business in relation to her mother or that he was conducting business in a way he didn't want his wife to aware of. Whatever the reason, William continued to keep information from his wife all through their marriage.

The year 1783 also brought more disturbing news, this time from William's father. During a visit to Blount Hall in December, William learned that his stepmother was gravely ill. Though this woman had a part in raising William, he says nothing in his writings; she died soon after his visit. William quickly returned to his business matters without a further word of concern.

Another land-grabbing opportunity came up, and he decided to travel south again to take advantage of the opportune timing. He left Piney Grove in December of 1783, heading for Wilmington and Georgia. Having decided not to take Molsey along, he stopped off in Wilmington to pick up Molsey's brother Billy. Molsey's younger brother, William Grainger, was twenty years old and eager to join his brother-in-law on an adventure to Georgia.

These further travels through the South worked to further William Blount's political ambitions. He was able to keep in touch with the common man and meet with prominent gentlemen while on his way to Georgia to convince the state's government to give him a grant for the Muscle Shoals land owned by the state of North Carolina.

He had left his pregnant wife behind, not returning home for six months until sometime in the month of June 1784. Historians can only guess on the birth date of the Blounts' fourth child. Lacking a recorded month for the child's birth, historians have been left counting their fingers and toes or just plain guessing when the birth happened. It is entirely possible that Molsey gave birth to her fourth child during her husband's absence. Molsey could well have become pregnant when William returned in March of 1783. With that in mind, William Grainger Blount's birth would have occurred in early 1784 while his father, William, was in Georgia.

7

September 1785— Piney Grove, North Carolina

No matter what, she would survive this storm. She kept whispering this to herself over and over in an attempt to still the frantic beating of her heart. She cowered in the dank, dark cellar with her mother, clutching little Billy tightly in her arms, desperate to locate Sall and Hagar. She peered through a jagged hole in the house's foundation, the hole's edges starkly defined in the thunder and lightning flashes that screamed with the wails of the wind. The blasts of wind pelted the bricks as the driving rain blotted out her vision. Her keen sense of safety was drowning in her overwhelming fear of being crushed in the rubble of her home. The large white oak had come crashing down, pummeled by the fiercely howling winds, destroying the slaves' quarters. Now the voracious storm sought to devour the old magnolia tree beside the house.

Little Billy's wailing cries competed with the gale's shrieking. His miniscule fingernails dug into his mother's neck as he screamed for comfort that never came. Molsey did her best to console him, but nothing eased the poor little guy's fear and panic. Trapped inside the cellar, they were all at the mercy of the assaulting tempest. The house groaned and creaked against the cyclone's attack. Shutters slammed against the windows, and a deep-seated fear hunkered down in her soul. She had watched the menacing cloud earlier that day, their dark, ominous billows heralding an oncoming onslaught. The wind had risen hours ago, building to a force that knocked Hagar to the ground while the faithful slave had run to the slave quarters. Now she couldn't see Hagar or Sall. She prayed fervently for their and the other slaves' safety.

The seemingly endless storm dragged itself into night. Billy, who'd exhausted himself with his screaming and fear, was sleeping fitfully beside his mother. Molsey was quiet and worried. The house still stood, and her courage crept back like a guilty child returning to its mother. She cautiously carried Billy up the concrete cellar steps, drenched in the pooling water that spilled down into the cellar. Her mother followed hesitantly in her footsteps, eyes wide and questioning. Carrying Billy's tired little body and weighed down with the beginning realization of the damage, Molsey began to cry with the flood of relief that swept over her.

In the dimness and shadows, she barely made out the wreckage of the slave cabins shrouded in the leaves and branches splayed across the yard. Shutters, ripped from the house, lay scattered on the ground, much like her terror lay scattered about her whole being. A corner of the roof was altogether gone. At least the house still stood. What of Hagar and Sall and the other slaves? Stepping gingerly over the debris, she began to call out for them by name, with tense hope. The lingering wind swept their names from her lips. She called again. From the dark shadows of the night, a weak reply came to her eager ears. They were alive! The tree that had fallen on the slaves' houses had not taken the lives of her favored slaves.

Collapsing on the torn porch, she rocked her child in her arms. There were missing floodboards and the railing had folded in on itself, as tattered as the fragments of her thoughts. She was too weak to stand. Her mother walked slowly over to her and sat down in the rubble, wiping the grit from her eyes and straightening a stray strand of hair. Darkness sat with them, prodding them to do something, fix something, or pick up something. Molsey stood wearily with Billy in her arms and turned around. She stared back into a house that no longer looked like her home.

The next day's sunlight made nothing better. Molsey knew, with a renewed sense of purpose, that it was she and she alone who would have to rebuild these lives after that horrific storm. William, once more away on business, could not help. It wasn't long before news of her neighbors' lost roofs, livestock, and carriages made its way to her. Some barns had been literally uprooted, and quite a few residents were injured. Fortunately, none of the slaves had died in the rubble of their cabins, though several suffered grievous wounds. Hagar, Sall, Venice, and other domestic servants suffered mostly from the lingering, stalking fear of being blown away. Molsey busied herself with reassuring them all that the cabins would be repaired or replaced and the crops replanted.

Her own home was at the top of the list for repairs. She ordered Sam, renowned for his skill in carpentry, to fix the roof and nail the shutters back in their places. Other slaves were set to clearing out debris around the plantation, but who would clean up the debris in her mind concerning her husband's absence during such a terrible nightmarish time and its subsequent crisis? She couldn't help but resent being left behind, alone, to repair this world they called Piney Grove. The memory of his determination to leave before she could be ready to go with him dogged her thoughts, feeding her resentment and anger. She harbored a particular bitterness concerning their parting argument. Why was he so adamant of her capability when she felt so incapable? At the age of twenty-four, she couldn't help feeling there was so much more she needed to know about plantation life, political life, and her own life.

The incessant chatter within her mind grew louder and louder, telling her she'd regret it if she tried to handle things by herself. But slowly, ever so slowly, self-pity transformed into a fierce determination to prove to him—to herself—that she could and would do it! Dismissing the intrusive chatter like she would a prattling child, she turned around to assess all that was hers—that was theirs. If William was determined to become rich and

85

powerful, she would be too. She tilted her chin up, a flash of defiance and determination in her eyes, embracing the newfound flush of self-fulfillment. Gazing over the carnage spread across the land, she saw it anew. The storm and its spent fury was teaching her, showing her what she must do to become the strong, sophisticated, and influential woman she was meant to be. Never again would the storm of separation bruise and batter her soul.

ᘠ⅌⅌⅌ᘡ

Storms that beat down upon the coastlands of North Carolina were notorious for the damage and loss of life they left in their wake. Such storms were not called hurricanes since that term had yet to be coined. Ever since 1900, records indicate how North Carolina has been a gifted recipient of these storms. Due to the way the coastline protrudes into the Atlantic Ocean, the Tar Heel state has long been vulnerable to these direct strikes. When a hurricane crept in from the ocean and crossed the land, its winds would lessen, often spawning tornados. This double weather phenomenon guaranteed the destruction of crops, livestock, and homes. By the time a hurricane reached New Bern, Piney Grove, or Masonborough, winds could still have been racing at over one hundred miles per hour, along with accompanying tornados.

Though hurricanes were not tracked in 1785, journal and diary entries indicate the occasions of these terrible storms. Blount family records and letters tell tales of how several of their merchant brigs sank due to these fierce storms, particularly in the Caribbean. With no way to forecast the weather, North Carolina residents were left to read signs of nature the best they could while not really knowing of the strength of a storm until it was literally upon them. Cellars were the only shelters available since storm shelters didn't exist. It is sound testimony to the sturdy construction of colonial homes of the rich that they endured throughout such storm-ravaged seasons for centuries. An excellent example of this was found in Blount Hall. Built about 1762, it stood firm until the 1960s until it burned down, having weathered a multitude of such storms.

Molsey had decided that she would have to meet the storms of her life without having her husband beside her. She had only recently weathered the birth of yet another child without William by her side, a son born in the spring of 1784. Named for his father and mother, he was christened William Grainger Blount, soon nicknamed Billy. As the first surviving son of the popular politician and land speculator, he was welcomed into the family as all firstborn boys were greeted. Now William had an heir. This little boy also represented a turning point for Molsey. She now had a son who would care for her in her old age.

She clung tightly to the happiness of having a little boy, as did William, but intrusive fears rushed in, distilling the happiness. Only a year had passed since her sister-in-law Mary Baker Blount, wife to William's brother Thomas, had died in childbirth, nine months after their marriage. Thomas's newborn son had also died. The memory of her little Cornelius disturbed her brief moment of happiness. Having experienced the delicate balance between life and death in childbirth, Molsey most likely contended with the possible outcomes of each new pregnancy and birth.

William seemed undisturbed by the seasons of life and death. His commitments to business affairs and political ambitions were all-consuming. He remained closer to home through what was left of 1784 but prepared to leave for Georgia in the fall of 1785. At first he considered taking his wife and children with him but ultimately decided against it due to inerrant uncertainties. The growing problem with the Indians, as well as the future of western North Carolina, which would eventually become Tennessee, was uppermost in his mind. The Spanish informed the Americans in 1784 that any United States ship using the Mississippi River would be seized. Spain's announcement of their sole right of passage upon the Mississippi River was a precursor to William's future difficulties with Congress, eventually besmirching his future reputation.

William had been a delegate to the Continental Congress in 1782. This allowed him to position himself for inclusion in the Constitutional Convention of 1787. As a state assemblyman of North Carolina, he was involved in several issues that the state was wrestling with during the late 1780s. He worked hard to introduce bills regarding land ownership, something he fervently wanted, particularly the Land Grab Act. He sided with Congress's concern with white encroachments onto Indian lands, which had brought about problems with the Cherokee, Choctaw, and Chickasaw tribes. Another state dilemma concerned dissident citizens who had conspired to form the State of Franklin without the approval of the politicians in eastern North Carolina. Those residents ceded from North Carolina, only to abandon their efforts of statehood four years later.

While he was preparing to leave his family once more to head out for the Continental Congress of 1785, the Congress redirected him to Georgia. They needed someone to negotiate a new treaty with the Southern tribes, a negotiation that would be known as the Treaty of Hopewell, and chose him as their man. This treaty was complicated for both the settlers as well as the Indians. In the end, the Indians would lose again.

Before he left, William mentioned his intention to build a new house for his family in New Bern. In a letter penned to his brother John, he wrote of his decision to wait for construction until he had returned home. He refused to have a home built in his absence because he would not be able to oversee the work. A new house for Molsey meant another move and another refurnishing of a house, but she was ready for a larger house. As the family expanded, her dreams for a larger home were part of what William also wanted.

He was to be gone for months, another time of adjustment and determination for his wife. William was leaving to try and reach a treaty with the Indians, a position appointed by Gov. Richard Caswell and the United States Congress. This adventure would leave him in the woods for more than six months. As he stated to his brother in volume 1 of the *John Gray Blount Papers* (Winston

Printing Company 1952), "No Man was ever more tired of laying on Blanketts and Being in the Woods or more anxious to get Home than I am." He would not complete his duties to his government or return to Piney Grove until February 1786.

During the years between the birth of Billy in the spring of 1784 and the birth of her fifth child in 1787, Molsey spent three years without being pregnant. For an extremely fertile and healthy woman, this protracted gap between pregnancies signaled a change in the Blounts' relationship. As previously indicated, she gave birth within a year of her marriage and roughly every second year after that. Fertility wasn't a problem for this young wife. By the time she was twenty-three, she had been pregnant four times, leaving her with three surviving children in 1784. Her firstborn had died, and her second child, Nancy, was living with relatives. The exact date of when her third child, Louisa, joined Nancy is unknown but occurred when both were young. By the year William left for Georgia for his six-month adventure, it seems Molsey and her fourth child, Billy, lived at home with her mother.

The delay in having another child could be based on William's ongoing absences. Between 1784 and 1787, he was constantly on the move, remaining at home for only a few months and then leaving again. However, he was home for more than six months in 1785, without a child born in 1785 or 1786, begging the question, What happened?

Sometimes the cost of having a child could prevent a pregnancy, but the Blounts were far from poor; they were not even struggling financially. They were affluent, with a growing income. Could there have been a miscarriage? One historian has suggested that without providing concrete evidence to support that position. Was there a problem in their intimate life or emotional relationship? Perhaps, but again the assumption does not answer the question. Intimate affairs between couples can be difficult to decipher, and in this case only speculations can provide any plausible answer.

Birth control during the colonial years in North Carolina was similar to others areas of the American states. Preventing births is something people have attempted to do for thousands of years. Women, historically, have proven very inventive when it comes to avoiding pregnancy, using all sorts of concoctions and potions made from things like olive oil, pomegranate pulp, tobacco juice, or herbs to try to block conception. Women have sometimes controlled conception through the use of creative barriers inserted in the vagina, such as pessaries or diaphragms. Potions were sometimes made to drink in order to stimulate an abortion. Common among most couples was coitus interruptus (withdrawal) during intercourse or the ever-reliable abstinence.

Rather than focus on why Molsey did not have children at that time, it's best to consider what she was able to do. Without the burden of pregnancy and another child to handle, she was able to create a different sort of life for herself. Being a mother had brought fulfillment to Molsey, yet it also had brought pain and loss, death and empty arms. She lost her first son to death, her second child to a relative, and her third child would soon join her sister, leaving her with one child in 1785. After all this scrutiny, there is the simple knowledge that Molsey did not produce a living child in these years. Her next child would live only a few years.

8

November 1788—
Greenville, North Carolina

The ebony-draped funeral hearse creaked its way along the ancient tree-lined road. The horses' snorting interrupted the clouds of her grief, irritatingly distracting and comforting at the same time. Horses had always been a solace to Molsey in distressful times. The cadence of their hooves on the road stirred up memories of past funerals. These memories were quickly reined in by bilious rising sensations of dread and trepidation. How she loathed funerals! Her mind raced to decipher some meaning from this most recent death. She sighed, returning to the eternal truth that life and death were but parts of the natural, inevitable stages of life. Resigned, she walked slowly behind the hearse, needing her husband beside her. Her head bowed heavily beneath the weight of thought and concern.

The death of her sister-in-law, Louisa Blackledge, placed her own mortality in the forefront of her mind. Her own dreaded fears of childbirth and death swirled in her head as she stumbled on a small stone, reaching out instinctively to steady herself. Louisa had been wed but a couple of years. She and Richard had held such dreams and hopes for their new home in Tarborough. Those dreams had all come crashing down with her death.

The hearse slowly rolled into the church's graveyard, the headstones silent sentries waiting for an army to pass in review. Molsey glanced at names engraved on the tombstones. "Abigail, wife of Thomas" and "Virginia, daughter of Elijah and Mary Roberts"—all women she had known, all dead and gone. Turning from those names carved in stone and eternity, she forced herself to think of her own family. Richard stood beside her, watching his deceased wife's casket as it was removed from the hearse. He glanced quickly at Molsey for some sign of reassurance and support. The loss of his wife, Louisa, had been a shock to the whole family. Molsey recalled how unsettled William had been at her death. Louisa was the first of her husband's siblings to die. She'd been only thirty-three years old.

Richard, the grieving widower, walked quietly to his wife's coffin, looking to straighten the wrinkled black pall, which had been so lovingly laid over the coffin at the start of this dismal journey. But the uncooperative wind insisted on lifting a corner, exposing the walnut wood beneath its slight bluster as he tried in vain to smooth it out once more. Molsey stepped forward, adding her hand to his as she aided in the smoothing replacement of the drape. How do you straighten out an untimely death? How do you smooth out the wrinkles of such a loss? She stepped back from the hearse, noting the hundreds of mourners who came to gather with the family at the grave site.

The simple ceremony ended, but her tears refused to. She recalled the sudden death, five years ago, of her sister-in-law Mary Blount during childbirth, along with the death of Mary's infant son. Her sweet smile and gentle way had remained with Molsey ever since. Then her thoughts returned to Louisa, mourning the loss of the gaiety and friendship she had nurtured within their family. In her mind's eye, she could see Louisa gamboling with her children, most especially the youngest one. Louisa never forgot to bring them special toys from her trips to Raleigh or New Bern. She recalled the numberless times Louisa had taken them on carriage rides and walks to the general store for candy. They never failed to be enthralled by her stories about giants, princesses, and the Pilgrims. Then an image flashed in her mind—the horrid memory of the death of Billy, her younger brother. She forced the memory of that early death from her mind; there just wasn't any room for it right now. Molsey wondered how she could ever explain Louisa's death to her own children.

Upon leaving the cemetery, the mourning adjourned to Blount Hall, though its tone mellowed significantly in the joining of friends and family who gathered to share stories of Louisa and to eat the home-cooked delicacies spread over long tables set out on the lawn. She so missed her William, wondering exactly where he was right now. While the mourners mulled about the cider and wine table, Richard began to pass out two silver spoons in gratitude to family members who had attended his wife through her illness and last days. These "coffin spoons" were popular with the recipients, and all were grateful. Sister Polly mentioned that she had recently used a pair of the spoons. Her ten-month-old son was teething, and the spoons brought some relief to his pain as he chewed and drooled on them. Molsey graciously received the spoons from Richard and wondered if they would be helpful with her own children.

Her thoughts abruptly turned to her children, and she glanced about, searching for them. The older cousins had been left to tend to the children during the funeral, and now she was uneasy, wondering where they were. Listening intently for childish chatter or laughter, she noticed little feet protruding from beneath the lacy tablecloth. Bending down, she picked up the frilly edge, her face brightening as she spied their curls and innocent smiles. They were all safe and thoroughly enjoying themselves. Standing upright, she brushed a wisp of hair from her eyes, pondering how to she could possibly keep her children safe. At the same time, she couldn't ignore the fact that so many illnesses and diseases were continually robbing life from these small children; so many died.

Her silent musing brought an image of her husband to mind, and she sighed, the all-too-familiar emptiness of his absence returning to her heart. It seemed he was always busy elsewhere whenever the family needed him. Births and deaths trampled others, but not her William. Family celebrations and crises were buried beneath mounds of political meetings, decisions, travels, votes, or business journeys to gain more land grants. Now he was in Fayetteville, engulfed in yet another political meeting and veto. Her life seemed to be forever changing; was she becoming more independent, or was she just becoming lonelier? No, she wasn't lonely—not exactly. She had her children. They fulfilled her sense of accomplishment and provided meaning to her life. But for all her clinging to her children, she couldn't keep them from leaving her.

✺✺✺✺

The year of 1788 was once more a difficult year for the Blounts, one of so many filled with tragedy, deaths, changes, and loss. And through it all, William and Molsey watched each other evolve into persons with different strengths and different longings. William grew even more politically powerful and longed for even more land, more fortunes. Molsey grew more independent and successful in managing her household and family, yet she longed to be closer and experience more companionship with William.

He was embroiled in politics. Along with his older brother John Gray, his cousin Abner Nash, his friend John Sitgreaves, and his lawyer, William went after another political appointment. Historian Masterson pointed out how he was also occupied with forming a nail factory and searching for more sources of corn, salt, and naval stores. His younger brother Thomas was returning from Europe, and there were ongoing problems with runaway slaves. Blount's interest in land was reaching a pivotal point as his attention turned to lands that would become the State of Tennessee. He became covetously absorbed in influencing the Federal government to appreciate the value of those lands.

Previously, in March of 1787, William Blount had ensured himself a place in the annals of history. He had been elected to represent North Carolina at the Constitutional Convention in Philadelphia. Arriving at the Convention on June 20, he stayed but a few days before heading south to New York to join the

Continental Congress in early July, after which he returned to Philadelphia, joining his political colleagues in the Assembly Room of the Pennsylvania State House, now known as Independence Hall. The newly written United States Constitution was signed in September of 1787. William's legibly bold and neat signature can be seen today, dominating the signatures of the other signers from North Carolina. Though signed, the Constitution would not go into effect until nine of the thirteen states had ratified it.

Upon William's return home, the subsequent conversations about the formation of the Constitution would surely have piqued Molsey's interest. As an educated and intelligent woman, her discernment regarding changes in government and her pride in her husband would have been fodder for discussion for weeks. On a more personal note, William returned home to welcome his second baby boy. Molsey held in her arms another little boy, born in 1787, possibly while Blount had been away at the Constitutional Convention.

There's not much recorded in history about this child. Most likely born sometime between February and July of 1787, the Blounts settled on an interesting name for their fifth child. They gave him the confusing name of Blount. His first name was Blount, and his last name was Blount. The naming of this little baby is awkward or redundant at best, creating many questions. Why in the world would they name a child such a confusing name? Without a middle name, or more information on his birth, his presence has confounded both genealogists and historians, yet the Blount family repeatedly named their children in a manner that raised an eyebrow here and there or caused a chuckle. It was a long-standing family tradition to name children after family members, famous people, or in a humorous manner. An excellent example of the Blount humor in baby names is seen in William's youngest brother's name. Born in 1771, his half brother was named Sharpe Blount and another brother was named Reading Blount.

With Molsey pregnant throughout the last part of 1786 and early 1787, her mother remained in residence to help, assisting at yet another birth. With Blount's birth, those children living at home included three-year-old Billy, newborn Blount, and possibly five-year-old Louisa. Nancy, seven, was living with Thomas and his sister Ann. Ann Blount Harvey had taken on the role within the Blount family of the one member who moved into the home of a relative in order to care for the grieving or those that needed special care. Thomas, now a widow, settled in Tarborough, and Ann moved in to help care for Nancy.

There was another change for William Blount's family that year. By June, William had moved his family to Greeneville, North Carolina, originally known as Martinsborough. After the Revolutionary War, the town had been renamed for the Patriot hero, General Nathanael Greene. Historians have described the town as a small courthouse village with several stores and wharves, a profitable place for Blount to carry on his businesses. Later, George Washington would state in his memoirs that Greenville was an "indifferent place." As a new resident of the town, Blount became one of the first trustees of the Pitt Academy, a school for boys.

He had originally planned on building a new house in New Bern for his family, but for some unknown reason, he moved his household to Greenville. It was an ideal choice for business reasons since he was now closer to his brothers John Gray and Thomas. John Gray lived approximately twenty-two miles southeast of William, along the Tar River in Washington, North Carolina, while Thomas was settling in Tarborough, about thirty miles to the northwest, also along the Tar River. The exact location of this latest family home is unknown. In fact, none of his homes in North Carolina survived development, progress, or the expansion of roadways. The only William Blount residence left in existence today is in Knoxville, Tennessee.

Moving to Greenville meant a larger house since apparently more than just family members were now living with Molsey and

William. Wards and apprentices were also housed within their mansion. During those colonial times, wealthy families would often take in wards or children that could not be cared for by their parents. Molsey would have had to agree to these arrangements since she would have been the person to most influence and care for a young ward.

William had been court appointed to care for young Abner Nash Jr., who later became a problem for him. William's friend Abner Nash had died, instructing the courts to make William the guardian of his young son. The *John Gray Blount Papers* reveal the nature of this young man's problem and personality. His mother "declares She can keep him no longer." In February of 1788, William wrote to his brother John Gray, pleading for help. It seemed nobody wanted this troublemaker in their home, especially Molsey, who had put her foot down. William told his brother, "...my Wife is much opposed to his living with me, and as T. Ogden is to live with me in the future I have hardly room for him and if I had I have not the Colour of Business for him." Molsey had her hands full with three children and the running of a household, plus the other social obligations of a politician's wife. She was not willing to be encumbered by a difficult child, one who had already resided with her earlier.

The fate of this child was not of interest to Molsey, but William was frantic to find a new home for this boy before he arrived in Greenville. He badgered his brother to take this problem off his hands. He attempted to bribe him with an offer to pay for the boy's board, suggesting several jobs this boy could do for John. Fearing the imminent arrival of this boy, he promised John that if he took the boy in before he came to Greenville, Abner might just be "...better than his Character for no Person could behave better than he did while with me a Week at Greenville." The fate of this young man is lost in the brothers' letters. It is doubtful that he found a home with the Blounts after William noted, "Forgive this attempt to impose on you a thing that I Know not what to do with and that no Body else will have..."

Though the Nash ward no longer lived with the Blounts, another ward moved in. Titus Ogden became a part of their household, probably around the age of ten. Being apprenticed to a wealthy landowner was common in the eighteenth century. It meant that a young boy would be able to learn a trade or a craft. In the Blount family, apprentices had a multitude of opportunities in learning such skills as managing a plantation, rotating crops, business strategies, shipping practices, and operating naval stores while also learning about the advantage of land ownership. A contract, signed between the aristocrat, the parents, and the child, could last up to ten years. Living at the Blount plantation for the duration of his apprenticeship, Titus Ogden became a part of their family life. He learned to read, write, and complete his sums and was fed and clothed by Molsey.

Continuing to appear in the Blount history, Titus Ogden completed his years of service to William. Upon his release from apprenticeship, he was free to pursue his own business as a merchant, having received a suit of clothes referred to as a freeman's suit and probably some tools. Unfortunately, history records his early death in October of 1793.

Molsey, William, and their family had moved into a new and larger home in Greenville. Unfortunately, the excitement and work involved in the move wouldn't last long. Molsey's brother Billy died sometime in 1788. While Billy traveled with William, he had grown closer to his sister and her husband, frequently staying at Piney Grove or in Greenville between his trips with his brother-in-law. His loss had to have been devastating to Molsey and her mother. The details of his death and burial are unknown.

Sickness and death continued to hound Molsey. William complained to his brother John, as noted in the first volume of the *John Gray Blount Papers*, that in the early fall his mother-in-law "has been so indisposed that Molsey could not visit Halifax and she is yet in a bad Way not very sick but so much so as to keep her

Bed constantly." Approaching her fifty-ninth year, old age was creeping up on her. Mrs. Grainger had always been a concern for Molsey while living with her daughter. William had been left in charge of Mrs. Grainger's finances and legal issues while Molsey tended to the day-to-day care of her mother. Both women relied on the other during times of sickness or death.

November was an especially difficult month. Louisa Blount Blackledge, William's younger sister, died just two years after her marriage to a family friend of William and his brothers. The family was devastated by her death, as was her husband, Richard Blackledge. Louisa's family attended to her throughout her illness, though William was out of town often.

In early November, suspecting she didn't have long to live, Louisa made out her last will and testament. Having no children of her own, she had obviously grown very fond of Molsey's little boy Blount, mentioning him in her will. Though the boy was but one year old, Louisa had him and his future on her mind. She left nothing to Molsey or William, but toddler Blount became a landowner, like his father, at the tender age of one. Her will read in part:

> I give and bequeath unto my loving Nephew Blount Blount, Son of William Blount two Lotts of Ground in the Town of Tarborough, known and distinguished in the Plan of the said Town by Number One Hundred and Four and Number One Hundred and Five (N 104 & 105) with all and Singular the Appurtenances thereunto belonging or in any wise appertaining to him his Heirs and Assigns forever.

December, the last month of 1788, brought no relief. William rode off on his various travels throughout North Carolina as a businessman and lawyer for his family. His trip to Wilmington and his frustration with his responsibilities was a constant source of irritation between him and Molsey. Though she occasionally traveled with him on short journeys, he chose to leave her behind in December. Again, the *John Gray Blount Papers* inform us about William's frustrations. While in Fayetteville early in the month, William firmly stated, "I go from this to Wilmington on Business respecting the Estate of Caleb & Will Grainger, & my own and must I see clearly at all Events go Shortly to Georgia about this damned Indian Treaty Affair."

During his absence, he was well aware that Molsey was upset with him. As he had done before, he wrote to his brothers, asking them to help him in somehow appeasing his wife. Molsey was apparently upset with his frequent absences, and William chose to indirectly deal with this. In the historical family letters of the *John Gray Blount Papers*, he asked his ever-faithful brother John to intervene. "Pray inquire what Molsey may want and supply her for I suppose She will be enough dissatisfied at my Absence." Blount left for Wilmington, hoping his brother could assuage Molsey's anger.

William's request for his brother's help with his wife indicated a problem in their marriage. Without any input from Molsey through any sort of historical record of her own, through a diary or communication with others, only William's viewpoint is available. His banter often revealed his need to hide what he was really doing from his wife. As recorded in the *John Gray Blount Papers*, he had told his brother in the past to allay Molsey's discontent with "some good excuse for me." During his absences, he wrote letters to his brother to give to Molsey instead of writing directly to her. He rarely saw her as confident or capable when he wasn't there.

The letter from Fayetteville was the first indication that Molsey was becoming more irritated with William and possibly more independent. Lacking honesty from her husband in regard to his travels, motives, and movements, she was left to manage the Blount family and plantation on her own. She had put her foot down, refusing to accept a certain ward into the family. Perhaps she was weary of William's neglect or dishonesty toward her, forcing her to become more assertive.

In studying Molsey's life, it is sometimes difficult to discern the truth about her marriage. Without journals, diaries, and letters Molsey might have written, it is difficult to comprehend the true character and personality of this historical figure. With a keen eye on colonial culture and society, the reader can begin to evaluate the possible consequences in a marriage where one spouse is frequently absent or dishonest. For an intelligent, educated, well-mannered, aristocratic lady like Molsey, it's not difficult to imagine that at this point of her life, she decidedly became more distant as she became more confident. At the age of twenty-seven she realized just how alone she really was and, out of necessity, began to develop a more autonomous life.

William, alone in his travels, was experiencing his own set of complexities. Molsey received news of them from her brother-in-law John Gray. While making his way to Wilmington, William lodged at an inn called Dekeysers. In the first week of December, the inn caught fire. William related to his brother in the first volume of the *John Gray Blount Papers* how the fire had burned "part of my Clothes of which I had none to spare as well as a part of John P. Williams who was my fellow Lodger and the flames got to such a height that it was with much difficulty the House was saved." While William was recovering from that ordeal, he suffered a carriage accident the very next evening. Apparently unhurt, he bragged of having been thrown ten feet without being injured.

The year ended with William returning to Greenville rather than going on to Georgia. Perhaps he hurried home intent on mending his relationship with his wife or to better prepare for his next journey. Molsey and William's marriage would endure his long absences, and each spouse was changing because of them. For Molsey, the future was constantly shifting, demanding more courage and forbearance from her. By the end of 1788, she was again with child.

9

April 1790—
Greenville, North Carolina

She seethed with fury. Pacing up and down the hardwood floor, her long dark green dress inhibited her stride. She twisted her hands before her, her vitriolic words spitting out at him.

"How could you do this? How?" she screamed. She spun about before the fireplace, grabbed the ornate Chinese vase, and threw it at him. It shattered on the floor. "You don't care what happens to your family! All you care about is more land, more attention, more power!" she shrieked, her flashing dark blue eyes darting about the room.

William interrupted her best he could, speedily explaining, "Now, Molsey, you know that isn't true. Why, I love my family. Just look what I have provided for you—a gorgeous home, the finest furniture, beautiful horses and whatever you need."

She blinked in shock of what she'd just heard, shaking her head in disbelief. Her vision cleared as the rage melted away. She now realized just how different they were, each seeing life through different eyes. She froze midsentence, saying not a word, locked in silence.

All she had ever wanted was for her family to be together, to soak in moments of shared laughter and hours of amiable companionship. She wanted nothing more than to have William home with her and the children. Yet here he was, leaving on an extended trip over the mountains to some obscure part of North Carolina for God only knew how long, and he had the audacity to inform her—not ask her, mind you—that he expected his family to follow, to be with him. Absolutely impossible! How could he even think of taking his children—their babies, her mother, and her—to that untamed, wild frontier, to those dark forests filled with deadly savages and fierce Indians?

Molsey silently and purposefully strode from the room, holding her head high, kicking the shards of porcelain out of her way. She was adamant. She refused to leave Greenville, would never leave her friends and family or this beautiful plantation. William ran after her, grabbing her by the hand and spinning her to face him. His hands grasped her firmly by her shoulders as she struggled to evade his touch. In a calm, insistent voice that brooked no reproach, he told her, "I am leaving, and you will follow. You have plenty of time to consider how you want to do that, but you are leaving. This appointment is very important to the country, to this family, and to me. Do you understand?"

She understood. Once more, she was being left behind. Molsey stumbled from the porch. William watched her go, shaking his head in frustration, impatient with his wife. He knew that he must convince her about this opportunity. He was certain to be selected by Congress and President Washington for the post of the first Governor of the Territory South of the River Ohio. Such an opportunity was certain to seal his future as an influential man in the historical annals of this foundling nation. It would also ensure his fortune from the lands west of the mountains—his lands, lands he had attained through speculation and grants. William took a long breath, easing the stress from his mind. He would give her time. He would figure out a way to assure her of the wisdom of this move. Persuading Molsey had always been easy.

Molsey spotted Belle in the pasture, grazing on some dried grass beneath the huge white oak. Hearing the creak of the gate as it was opened and hearing Molsey's call, Belle lifted her head, losing all interest in foraging. Reaching for Belle's silky neck, Molsey desperately hugged her and released the tears. Belle was her comfort, her stabilizer when she was grieving, lost, feeling indecisive, or confused. Nuzzling the horse's soft muzzle and glistening cheek usually never failed to melt away all the hurt and pain—not this time, though. A flood of bitter tears of frustration and hurt cascaded heatedly down her cheeks. Belle stood patiently, nickering in response to her sobs. Her tears slowly abating, Molsey stood back, patting her friend affectionately as she slowly reined in her emotions.

Her thoughts spilled from her lips. "Maybe he won't go. Maybe I can get him to stay." She reassured herself that surely he cared enough about her, that he wouldn't go if she didn't. Her brow furrowed, her mind fretting over the safety of her children. She recalled the recent tales she'd heard about Indian attacks—how brutal, animalistic savages slaughtered even women and children. Surely now that she was expecting another baby, William would think twice before exposing her and their children to such peril.

The next morning, sharing a sumptuous breakfast with her and the children, William departed with John Allen and Abner. Molsey waved him off with a sweep of her hand, her mind already turning to the more immediate tasks of the household and care of the children. She deliberately put away thoughts about William's declaration until later. For now, while the house slaves dusted and swept, she tended to the feeding of Richard, her youngest. Born the previous year, he was just starting to toddle around on his strong little feet. His brothers, Billy and Blount, were happy to tease when he fell down, but sweet Louisa, his older sister, always helped him up when she visited. Richard had those dark blue eyes of his mother and his father's blond locks. Molsey's life revolved around her children, including the one on the way, not due for several months yet according to her calculations.

She brooded over her husband as she went about the household chores. William had not been home when Richard had been born. Instead, he didn't meet his sweet new son until he had returned from a trip to Halifax, New Bern, and Edenton. William had cuddled with him for hours, counting his perfect little toes and fingers over and over. Molsey held no delusions concerning the fact that William's future meant he would always be traveling far from home. She was smart enough to understand that as a statesman with an eye on an even higher office and status in the new government, William would continue his forays around the southeast until he could no longer physically walk or sit in a carriage.

She knew how much her husband loved being part of the heartbeat of this new nation; it was so much a part of who he was that without it he wouldn't be the man she so adored and needed. He would get together with President George Washington or John Adams whenever he could. Acknowledging that unalterable precept of her husband's character, she began—albeit reluctantly—wondering what life on the frontier would be like. Thoughts of unchartered, undeveloped wilderness plagued her soul, along with thoughts of brutal, painted, half-naked Cherokee and Chickasaw warriors lurking behind every tree and boulder, causing tremors to shiver up her arms and back. The lack of merchants or a church or a bookseller unsettled her mind as well. She would be leaving so much behind.

Her youngest babe began to cry, undeniably hungry, triggering a visible response in Molsey's body as she bundled him to her breast to nurse. Cradling her son in the safety of her arms, she held tight to the hope of a future for her child, one that involved his safety and well-being in Greenville. She backed up to a rocking chair, settling comfortably in its seat. Richard instinctually nuzzled his mother, finding the nourishment he craved. Molsey's slender fingers absentmindedly stroked his silken golden hair, wondering how she might be able to stay if William left. She admitted that she needed him. She would have to go. Shaking her head under the frown that wrinkled her brow and turned the edges of her mouth downward, she considered the difficulties behind this new situation, this new change, as she went on stroking her son's hair. Could she somehow keep her children safe?

The appointment of William Blount as the Governor of the Territory South of the River Ohio in 1790 was the pinnacle of his political career but a frightening unknown threat to Molsey. At home with all the comforts and luxuries of the aristocratic lifestyle she had become accustomed to, Molsey saw this governor's position as a threat to her family's stability and safety. To move from the security of friends, family, and modern conveniences like the new spinning wheels, theaters, bookstores and her beloved home was unthinkable. The rumors and stories she'd heard about dangerous and life-threatening Indians on the other side of the mountains caused her hours of distress, and even nightmares. All William understood was that this change meant, "The salary is handsome, and my western lands had become so great an object to me that it had become absolutely necessary that I should go to the western country." He was ecstatic. He would be living closer to his vast land holdings. Mr. William Blount would eventually own millions of acres of land, the exact amount still unknown.

Since he was not a frontiersman, but an educated and cultured gentleman, this appointment was an adventure that took him into uncharted territory in more ways than one. He had been appointed not only Governor of these frontier lands but also superintendent of Indian Affairs. His jurisdiction stretched from the Appalachian Mountains to the Mississippi River, the future states of Kentucky and Tennessee. Blount would have to become adept in balancing two conflicting political positions. As America expanded the frontier, settlers demanded more land, the Indians demanded protection from white encroachment.

By late March of 1790 William learned that he was assured of the coveted appointments in the ceded lands of North Carolina. By June, it became official; Congress approved the position and announced it. He had to be ready to leave for his new position within months. However, he faced the daunting job of convincing Molsey that the whole family would be moving to the frontier. The historical record convincingly declares that Molsey was distressed when she realized the impact of this journey on her family but not that she wept for three days. She certainly was upset, faced with a dangerous move west, and especially now that she might be pregnant again. Another child would increase the danger and burden of the other travelers as well herself. Her youngest was less than a year old and her oldest child, Nancy was ten.

Looking back to 1789, the birth of Richard Blackledge, the sixth child and third son of William and Molsey Blount, barely entered the family records. He had been named for William's friend and deceased sister's husband, Richard Blackledge. This newest son was born on May 8, 1789, in Greenville during a time of pestilence, death, and political upheaval. Yellow fever stalked the residents of the lowlands. Relatives were dying everywhere. And all the while, William continued to pursue political power, the purchase of more land, and the development of more businesses.

Masterson further examines Mr. Blount's actions. "He sought to recover estates for business clients, dunned for debt collections, sold cargoes from the West Indies, and found farms and positions for the numerous Harvey family connections." William Blount had become the "recognized champion of Western speculators and of the West." Even so, many of his motives and actions were questionable. Some viewed him as a dishonest man while others believed him brilliant and masterful in business. Historians themselves have not been able to decide if his land dealings were completely trustworthy or not, and questions remain about that even to this day. Why did he use aliases in several of his land transactions? William Saunders asks hard questions also in the *Colonial Record of North Carolina, Volume 10* (1886). How was he able to be in "possession of real estate that he wasn't entitled to," and why had "he wheedled the Indians out of their lands." It's unclear as to whether Molsey knew of these dishonest practices or not.

Molsey remained steadfastly focused on her family and life on the plantation during 1789 and into 1790, fully aware of the future move west. Caring for the children along with the family's wards, seeing to the preparation of food, and overseeing the indentured servants and slaves, along with educating her children in faith and morals, kept her busy. Teaching her children little verses, manners, courtesy, and a love of literature was an important part of Molsey's role as a mother. As her children grew, a teacher was hired for the boys. The two sisters, Nancy and Louisa, would learn their letters and manners with Thomas Blount and Ann Harvey. The girls would surely be taught in all manner of things important for young ladies to know.

The year 1789 was far from being pleasant. During the summer another yellow fever epidemic threatened the lives of the residents along the eastern coast of the United States. Transmitted by mosquitoes, yellow jack thrived in North Carolina. Everyone was well aware that diseases lurked in the buzz or hum of every mosquito and its bite. Colonists planted pennyroyal about the foundations of their homes to repel the pestiferous pests. Now preventable, it was known as the most infectious and fatal disease of its kind during colonial times. Symptoms included high fevers, chills, nausea, muscle pain, and loss of appetite, followed by liver damage with jaundice, hence the name yellow fever. Malaria was another deadly fever. Also transmitted by mosquito, summers became periods of dread and death.

On August 17, 1789, at the age of sixty-three, the patriarch of the Blount family died. Jacob Blount was said to have died from a nervous fever. Such a diagnosis could refer to any number of fevers. Since malaria and yellow fever was epidemic in the area of Blount Hall at the time, it is highly likely he died from one of those diseases. He had outlived two of his three wives, having recently married the third. His death heralded a period of great sorrow over the loss of a popular and renowned planter, landholder, and revolutionary war soldier. His skill in politics and business were his legacy to his sons. His obituary allows us a glimpse of his personality:

> Independent in his sentiments and steady in his
> resolutions, he abeyed the impulse of his own mind and
> by always doing that which appeared to him right,
> obtained the friendship of many, and the esteem and
> respect of all who knew him. It would be difficult to
> determine whether his hospitality was more general or
> liberal at all times his doors were alike open to the poor
> and to the rich, the distressed, the weary, and the sick
> traveler, were sure to find a home at Blount Hall.

The ultimate compliment was written at the end of the obituary: "…he was, 'The noblest work of God, an HONEST MAN.'"

After Jacob Blount died, Molsey, her sisters-in-law, Mary (Mrs. John Gray) Blount and Sukey (Mrs. Jacob) Blount, were extremely worried about the yellow fever's hold on the citizens of Edenton, Tarborough, and Greenville. In the early fall, Mary Blount wrote to Molsey:

> …I have heard they have bin very sickly & a number
> died with the yellow fever…" Other members of the
> family had also been sick. She shared how "Lucy (Mrs.
> Reading) Blount has not bin hear since you left this her
> Children as all had the Flux Carolina is the poorest
> Child, you ever saw but are getting better…

The flux or dysentery was an inflammatory disorder of the intestine. Its symptoms—diarrhea, mucus in the feces, dangerously high fever, and extreme pain—could leave a young child extremely debilitated and ill. Caused by contamination of food or drinking water, the illness could endure a minimum of a week, leaving the patient convalescing for a lengthy period of time. Lacking today's medical knowledge, colonial families were unaware of precautions they could take in order to prevent the spread of bacteria and viruses. Just the simple daily practice of washing hands could have saved numerous lives.

Another death intruded into William's life. His longtime friend and political ally, the Governor of North Carolina, Richard Caswell, died while the Assembly was in session in Fayetteville. His death threw the session into chaos, resulting in the recession of the Assembly. John Gray and William remained to make funeral arrangements for their close friend and partner. While these state funerary preparations extended William's time away from home, it also led to another bout of fever and ague for him. William did not tell Molsey about his illness while she waited not-so-patiently at home with Billy, Blount, and five-month-old Richard. He eventually returned home late December of 1789, still ill. He would continue to battle recurring malaria symptoms for the rest of his life.

However, it had not been just the fever and ague that kept him from going home. Rather, he chose to linger after the assembly had ended in an attempt to gain more money. Revealing a greedy side not usually seen, his attempt at gaining fraudulent funds was refused by a clerk. As Masterson tells it, Mr. Blount did not hurry home after the assembly adjourned because he "attempted to collect mileage as delegate to the ratification convention from the frontier Tennessee County, seeking fees for 750 miles coming and going." The clerk refused to pay the statesman, stating that, "In fact…did not travel…the miles he charges."

Sickness hounded the Blounts throughout the winter of 1789–1790. William continued to suffer from bouts of ague, along with a horrible cold and racking cough. Molsey had her hands full as the long-awaited spring of 1790 approached. However, her ill husband refused to stay home. His announcement in late March of his long-awaited move to the frontier wilderness foreshadowed another round of absences. William was determined to be an active part of the settlement of the new frontier, west of the mountains.

By 1790, the Blounts owned a total of thirty slaves. Every slave was well treated, and some even received an education, but all of them were property that William was proud of owning. Molsey

111

oversaw the domestic slaves, especially when her husband was gone. John Allen, William's trusted farm manager, managed the plantation slaves. Molsey also occupied herself with occasional carriage rides led by her paired dapple grays or with attending horse races with family members in Washington, North Carolina. She doted on her horses, owning more than William thought she needed. On the few occasions he was at home, she and William enjoyed the still-new American theater. At that time, the first American comedy entitled *The Contrast* made its rounds through the new states and was very popular. Molsey would also have indulged in the first American novel, *Power of Sympathy*, a book spoken of within many literary circles.

Molsey had grown to relish entertaining guests in their home. With unlimited resources and the best of china and silverware, she held dances and dinners for family as well as political allies. Being the aristocratic wife of an important politician and businessman earned her the admiration of neighbors, relatives, and statesmen. Guests admired her sumptuous entertaining and gracious dinners, all served in the congeniality and conviviality of true Southern hospitality and style. The most important meal of the day was served during the noon hours. Her dinners consisted of turkey, quail, venison, sweet potatoes, cheeses, hams, pumpkin pie or hasty pudding, and a good helping of apple butter on various breads or muffins. Moving to the frontier would not include this lavish style of entertainment.

William's difficulty in convincing Molsey that they were moving did nothing to slow his flurry of ambitious activities. He hurriedly began to settle his father's estate and distribute the funds and furniture to his heirs. He needed to arrange a journey of Blount ships to Jamaica in order to smuggle turpentine into the country. He continued in land transactions, laboring to wrap up family land grants and surveys before he left. Molsey was left with even less time with her husband and more stories of frontier violence, which included the scalping of white settlers. She organized carriage trips to visit friends and spend time with family in order to see her little girls and garner support in preparation for what might happen to her family during a move over the mountains.

When summer arrived, William was ready to leave. Molsey was pregnant again and letting out her dresses. Not knowing when to expect her husband's return, she agonized about yet another birth without her husband's hand to hold. History records how William saw his future as unlimited in relation to profits and power while Molsey's voice was silent. One can only speculate as to her true thoughts and feelings.

As was common during colonial days, a wife's position was subordinate to that of her husband. Little was said in regard to a woman's emotions at a time like this. Yet all women who have loved deeply, who have lost children, and who have been left waiting behind throughout a marriage, as Molsey had done, must come to an understanding at one time or another. They must steel themselves against these overwhelming emotions and feelings of hurt and loss, or they will be destroyed. Subsequently, it becomes preferable to see Molsey becoming more stouthearted, securing for herself a clearer sense of autonomy, something unique to a woman in the 1790s. For what she would have to endure in the next year and half, she had to become strong, determined, and self-sufficient.

William left in late summer of 1790, his travels meandering in a circuitous route to his final destination. He took with him his favorite slave, Jack, Hagar's son, bidding farewell to land, family, and friends. It wasn't long—by September—that Blount seemed troubled by his absence from Molsey. He writes to his brother John Gray in an attempt to comfort Molsey in his absence. "I should be glad of your being at Greene Ville as often as convenient and saying such Things in an indirect manner as might induce a disposition in Molsey to visit the ceded Territory at least in the Course of the next Spring for sooner I shall not be ready." He reminds John that he is counting on him: "...on you is my dependence to hear from my Family."

It would be more than a year before Molsey would find herself disposed to visiting the ceded territory.

Leaving Molsey behind with three children, her mother, and another child to be born in 1791, along with full responsibility for the house and plantation, would have made life very difficult for her. We do not know when she finally transitioned to agreeing to the move. Perhaps she was waiting for his return before making a decision or missing him in his absence, but either way, she became aware that she really had no choice but to move. She had more than enough to keep her occupied in his absence until the worst possible thing happened.

Little Blount died on October 29, 1790. He was three years old, apparently dying of yellow fever or malaria, though his uncle suggests it was worms that caused his untimely demise. Molsey was devastated and unwell for quite a spell. The boy's small corpse was carried to Blount Hall for burial by his uncles Willie, Sharpe, and Mr. Ogden, with Molsey unable to attend the funeral or burial. We can assume that her mother was her closest comfort. John Gray informed his brother of his son's death in a letter. He had been to Greenville to visit with family and check in on Molsey, a favor William often asked him to do while he was away. John Gray stated:

> About 12 o'clock I found your Son Blunt just expired of about 24 hours sickness supposed to be the Ague & fever Billy & Jacob also have the Ague but not dangerous...Molsey is unwell but I hope it arises only from Grief I think Blunts disorder must have been Worms. The Corps was this morning sent to Blunt Hall.

Molsey was again suffering through the horrible agony of losing a child. Death and disease had stolen another of her precious children from her. Life was unfair. As had happened before, Molsey was crippled by this death, staggering to bed, overcome by pain and agony. She was approximately six months pregnant when Blount died. She would have been aware of the unborn child's movement in her womb throughout her time of mourning, an ever-present reminder of the cycle of life. Her other children would have been alarmed; something awful had occurred. Young William was six and probably missed his playmate. His sisters, living with a relative, learned of their brother's death shortly after John Gray returned home to Washington.

Blount died at the time his father was leaving the western side of the mountains. His travels had taken him from Greenville to Raleigh, to Hillsborough, to Rockingham Springs, and back to Raleigh. His coach then headed north to visit George Washington at Mount Vernon in Alexandria, Virginia. From Washington's home, he and his slave Jack continued on to Philadelphia. With business wrapped up, he was now prepared to head out to Winchester, Virginia. He would take the wagon road southwest to Staunton, Botetourt County, to his final destination at William Cobb's house near Jonesborough. He had very little contact with his family during these travels and would not know of his young son's death until November or December of 1790.

Molsey waited all through that winter to hear from her husband. Communication was difficult on the frontier; mail was unreliable. William frequently wrote his brother, complaining that he had not received any mail from his family for months. What would the next year bring? Both Molsey and William found themselves alone, each desperately wanting to know about the other. He was hundreds of miles away, and she was lost in grief and miles away from any peace and her love.

10

Christmas 1791—Piney Flats, Territory South of the River Ohio

The chilly wind blew away her thoughts of home like so much chaff. Wrapped snug in a warm woolen blanket, Molsey held her infant Jacob close to her heart. His tiny nose, peeking out from the warmth, brought a sense of comfort to her on this endless bumpy road to somewhere. The steel-gray sky reminded her of hasty partings and the emptiness of longing. As she stared out the slit of the carriage's window curtain, she thought of all she had had to leave behind—her two girls Nancy and Louisa, her brothers, her mother, her beautiful plantation home and its gentle view, her horses, her friends, her in-laws, her life. Her thoughts drifted along, matching the rhythmical clopping of the horses' hooves. It had been so hard deciding what pieces of furniture could go and what had to stay or be given away. There had been myriads of details to work through before leaving the huge home in her mother's care. She had to sell some of the slaves and pack up her belongings; every little bit had been a rending of her soul, felt only by her. Wearily her thoughts returned to her sons.

Billy and Richard had been squabbling over a broken toy that neither really wanted but tried to keep as their own just out of sheer boredom and stress. The journey had been arduous and left them cranky. Seven-year-old Billy had become impatient with his two-year-old brother. Molsey reached over to settle them down and felt their cold hands. It was freezing in the carriage. The curtains did little to keep the wind's icy fingers out. The chill seeped into her bones, causing her nose and ears to numb with the freezing chill. The ride up into the Appalachian Mountains had been uncomfortable due to the drops in temperature and the blustery wind. Discounting her own discomfort, she had to keep her children warm first.

William, noting the boys' impatience, placed little Richard in his lap. In an attempt to entertain the child, he began regaling him a story about the Indians, the deer, and the turkeys. Richard tried to wriggle off his father's lap but soon settled down, listening. Billy, wide-eyed, leaned expectantly against his father. The story, as told by William, was meant to be one of excitement and adventure. It entertained the boys but not Molsey.

The thoughts of Indians and the pending life that awaited them on the frontier brought only fear and anxiety, not excitement and delight. Her head had been filled with countless tales of frontier women being captured and enslaved by Indians. She knew how some white children had been taken by the Cherokee, the Chickasaw, the Chickamauga, or the Creek and scalped. She envisioned her children being forced from her embrace, never to be heard from again. These thoughts speared her conscious mind as she held Jacob closer to herself. How could she possibly protect her children in this vast wilderness overflowing with savages and wild beasts? What was William thinking bringing them here?

They were on their way to William and Barsheba Cobb's home in Piney Flats, nestled in the mountains of Washington County. It was nigh to Christmastime, and William had promised a celebration upon their arrival. He had spent hours telling Molsey about the Cobbs' home, called Rocky Mount—about their hospitality, their kindness, and their delight in hosting the Blounts. This Christmas journey was to be a new and wondrous time. The thoughts of a crackling fire and a hot mug of steaming cider warmed Molsey's thoughts. She had always loved Christmastime. It was a time of noisy gatherings and splendid dinners with family and friends. Then she suddenly began to recall how very different this Christmas would be. A silent tear creased its way down her cheek as she turned away from William.

Her thoughts turned toward her mother, another person now absent from her life. Her mother had remained in their Greenville home to keep a watchful eye on her granddaughters in Tarborough and await her own adventure, but she would see her next year, or maybe even sooner. Molsey ached for her so much. Molsey had always counted on her mother for support through the hard times of her life. Now there were only strangers to count on. Sure, her favored slaves were with her, but it was her mother she needed the most. Molsey was certain her husband would be traveling in this new frontier, leaving the family and her—again.

She thought back to last year. William had been gone for almost a year and a half, a lifetime for her. She had both lost a child and given birth to a child, and he had not been there at either time to help her. She realized the importance of his new position as governor of the Territory South of the River Ohio. She was proud of his desire to help in the expansion of her country. His patriotism was admirable, but she was also quite aware of the high cost she paid in loving this man. She had given up her life in North Carolina with all its comforts to come to this wilderness—a wilderness that was fraught with Indians and danger, a wilderness that offered little comfort and warmth. She had given up the safety, security, and well-being that the plantation in Greenville had provided for her children and herself. All she had now was the cold wind, her children's cold hands, and the cold thoughts of the wilderness.

William did what he could to cheer his wife. Aware that she hadn't wanted to come to Piney Flats, he had promised her a home of her own in the town he had named Knoxville. In an attempt to garner her favor, he had bribed her with the guarantee of a house comparable to what she was leaving behind. William spent hours convincing her about how she would enjoy this new town. She still wasn't convinced. To be left behind was unconscionable. To follow him was unthinkable. This journey was the hardest one of her entire life. Her tolerance for the unknown was sadly lacking, let alone her eagerness. She wanted to be home more than she wanted the next breath.

Just as Molsey could not tolerate another mile in the carriage, William beckoned the driver to slow down. They were approaching William Cobb's home. The old wagon road had been frozen in places, muddy in others; it was rutted, rugged, and teeth jarring. Finally, Molsey heard the slowing of the horses' hooves, the creaking of the harness signaling a stop. Was this an ending or a beginning? A huge tree stood sentinel before the log home. As the carriage halted in front of the two-story house, William leaned out the window and waved to a man standing under the large elm tree that bordered the Cobb land. At last, they had reached their destination. After a month of traveling from Greenville, the Blounts had made it in time for Christmas at Rocky Mount.

Traveling had occupied much of William's days. He was as bone-weary as Molsey, but he wasn't about to let her know that. He had left Piney Flats on September 22, 1791, after requesting a leave of absence from his gubernatorial duties in the new territory. Returning to North Carolina in October, he straightaway loaded his family, slaves, and possessions onto wagons and headed back to Washington County. Bringing his family to the frontier was risky, but he chose to ignore the risk, preferring to focus on future rewards. Now they had arrived a bit later than expected. The Cobbs were delighted at William's return to Rocky Mount, especially for the Christmas holiday.

William and Barsheba Cobb approached the carriage, extending a warm, welcoming greeting. They had been waiting for the Blounts for weeks. When Blount had left, he had told them he would be back in November. With Christmas the next day after their arrival, Mrs. Cobb had planned a large family dinner and celebration. Now she would include the Governor and Mrs. Blount and their children. Barsheba walked briskly down the stone steps, pulling her shawl tight about her shoulders. William helped Molsey down from the carriage, holding baby Jacob. She straightened her skirt, attempting to brush out the wrinkles.

120

Looking up, Molsey noticed the warm smile on Barsheba's face. She extended her arms, embracing Molsey in a reassuring hug.

"Welcome to Rocky Mount, Mrs. Blount, and Christmas greetings," said Barsheba as she stepped back.

"Thank you. It's been such a long, cold journey. I need to get the children out of the cold," pleaded Molsey. Her long, cold journey had just begun.

∾ꙅꙅ)))ꙅ◠

December of 1791 was a turning point for Molsey and her children. Arriving at Piney Grove in Washington County, which was still part of North Carolina, she faced a new frontier, a new family, and a new way of life. William Blount was faced with returning to the burden of governing the frontier and convincing his wife that she and the children would be safe. He had planned on returning to the Cobb home for a temporary stay, hoping to help his family acclimate to the wilderness frontier. His family also included his half brother, Willie, his newly appointed personal secretary.

William had first arrived the previous year in October of 1790 to Rocky Mount, setting up his temporary government with the Cobbs. William Cobb owned the large mountain home in Piney Flats that he called Rocky Mount. As governor, he had engaged in months of doling out political positions and judgeships and creating new counties. William Cobb and William Blount had spent hours talking about the future of the Territory South of the River Ohio. They were close friends. Cobb was a wealthy farmer, invested solely in improving his own farm and land; he held no political aspirations. As historian Ramsey notes, Cobb was known as "no stranger to comfort and taste, nor unaccustomed to what, in that day, was called style." Cobb was known as a generous, caring, and extremely accommodating man, and his wife was known for her hospitality and graciousness.

Cobb was not a political threat to Blount. Blount was comfortable at the Cobbs' homestead. He left no reason as to why he chose Rocky Mount as the initial capital of the new territory. Perhaps because it was accessible to the frontier, lying at the fork of the Holston and Watauga Rivers, and it would only be temporary. The Cobbs' reputation could have been a factor also. William Cobb was a friend of Richard Caswell, the former governor of North Carolina, a statesman Blount had been close to, taking on the responsibility of his funeral arrangements. A recommendation by Caswell could have been reason enough for Blount to choose to stay with the Cobbs. Whatever the reason, the Cobbs encouraged him to stay and assisted him in setting up the first capital in their home. Officially, the area was called the Territory South of the River Ohio or, more familiarly named, Southwest Territory.

William Cobb had arrived in the Piney Flats country of Washington County twenty years before William Blount. The Cobb home was a hub of hospitality in the wilderness. Built along the old rutted stage road leading into the western part of North Carolina, the house nestled among huge stones at the top of a high foothill, thus named Rocky Mount. The road itself was an important artery from North Carolina to the frontier, one of two routes from Abington to White's Fort. It was not a tavern but rather a rest stop for stages and a change of horses. It was also known as a friendly place to spend the night if weary travelers needed the rest.

The home boasted of glass windows, a pine mantle, and paneled stairways. With seven rooms, it has been described as primitive yet self-sufficient, not ornate but comfortable. The log home served as a gathering place, a welcoming place for all travelers to stop and rest at on their way to the west. As a self-sufficient farm, it provisioned nails, shingles, food staples, flax, and cotton not only to the family but to others through limited trading. The Cobb home was perfect for establishing the capital of the new Southwest Territory.

Molsey arrived at Rocky Mount in the icy month of December of 1791, close to Christmas day. Apparently the Blounts were delayed since the Cobbs had been expecting them in November. Their exact date of arrival is unknown, only that it was near Christmas Day. The Blounts appreciated the Cobbs' legendary hospitality. The Blounts weren't the only guests at the Cobb home; several Cobb family members were staying with the Barsheba and William as well. It was an especially busy family holiday. Hosting the Governor and his family was an honor, even though it created some crowding in the living arrangements.

One only has to visit the restored Cobb home today to appreciate just how crowded it would have been. The home, one of the largest built in the area during the 1760s, was on the main wagon road and near the Watauga River. It was constructed with white oak logs with paned windows, boasting comfortable rooms and fireplaces upstairs and downstairs. Two upstairs bedchambers provided comfort and warmth for both family and guests. By 1791, only Barsheba and William Cobb lived in the home, leaving one of the bedchambers for the Blounts and one for the Cobb visitors. The upstairs bedchambers were accessed by a steep single set of stairs leading to the larger bedchamber with a fireplace and a window, something that William Blount had appreciated in his letters home during his first stay there.

The smaller bedchamber was accessed through the larger one. This arrangement would have proved daunting for the Cobbs and Blounts. Both families' privacy was inevitably compromised. Cathy Hellier mentioned in the magazine *Colonial Williamsburg* that privacy in the eighteenth century "was the privilege of the well-to-do." Sleeping in such close quarters, each family would have been well aware of the other's intimate lives. The cries of a baby, the laughter or quibbling of the young boys, or the nighttime noise of lovers would have been a shared experience. And then there was Willie, William's half brother and personal secretary. Where did he sleep?

Finding living quarters for all those guests for several months seems daunting to us today, but somehow they all managed. Willie, William, Molsey, and their children remained at Rocky Mount from late December of 1791 until March of 1792. The homestead would have become a lively, noisy, and somewhat cramped cabin. The Rocky Mount Museum publication *Rocky Mount Christmas* (1791) indicates that accommodating small children and a baby meant "rearranging furniture, changing sleeping arrangements for the Cobb family, extra cleaning, cooking, meat preparation (hunting, slaughtering) and possibly the making of clothing and play things for the Blount children." Christmas was a time of visiting friends, going to church, dancing, and dining—holiday traditions that are far less materialistic than they are today. Little importance was given to Christmas gifts for the children. It wouldn't be until the nineteenth century that Christmas became a magical time for children. Santa Claus would not appear until 1823, a result of Clement Moore's poem.

For the Cobb family, the Christmas arrival of their visitors signaled a large dinner and garlands and greens decorating the mantle and tables, possibly with mistletoe in vases or hanging on the walls. Holly or bay leaves could have adorned the room, but a Christmas tree was not a part of the holiday in the 1790s. A Christmas dinner celebrated in the Great Room of Rocky Mount would include beef, goose, ham or turkey, mincemeat pies, and brandied peaches. To complete the festive meal, wines, rum punches, or brandy would be served.

Molsey stayed busy with much to occupy her time at the Cobbs. Barsheba, older than her, most likely introduced her to local families, showed her the stores in Jonesborough, and invited grandchildren to Rocky Mount to play with Billy and Richard. Since Molsey had brought several of her slaves with her, their involvement in the care of the family and food preparation would also have been worked out among the Cobbs and Blounts. Molsey undoubtedly shared her concerns as well as her joys with Barsheba. She would have told Barsheba about her meeting President

George Washington during his trip through North Carolina in 1791, her love of horses, and how she missed her mother.

Molsey and her children stayed with the Cobbs until March of 1792. By then she was again pregnant. This would be her eighth child if it lived past infancy. Her children were now living on both sides of the mountains. Nancy (eleven) and Louisa (nine) had remained in Tarborough. William (seven), Richard (two), and Jacob (six months old) were at the Cobbs with William and Molsey.

History states that there were only two of their sons at the Cobbs. Lacking a historical notation as to which son did not make this journey, the observation is that all three boys made the journey. During that time, an infant's presence was not always recognized. In fact, in a colonial census, infants were generally not counted. This could have been due to the high rate of infant mortality, and usually a family wouldn't recognize the baby until it was older. Therefore, it's only logical to consider that all three Blount boys were with their parents in December of 1791. Little Jacob, only five or six months old at the time of their transition to Piney Flats, certainly would not have been left behind, but he could have been intentionally left off the record.

Jacob Blount's birth in the spring or summer of 1791, was another birth that William missed. Named for his paternal grandfather, Molsey gave birth to him shortly after the death of three-year-old Blount. William was staying at Rocky Mount by then, traveling throughout the new territory. Again, without Molsey's husband present, Mrs. Grainger or Hagar would have attended the birth. As midwife both woman had the experience and love that Molsey needed for a delivery of a healthy baby. Jacob's birth probably reminded thirty-year-old Molsey of her recently deceased son. It can be assumed that this latest birth compelled her to become even more enigmatic yet stronger.

Rocky Mount in Piney Flats today. This was the home of William and Barsheba Cobb that William Blount used as he established the government in the Territory South of the River Ohio in 1790–1792.

William's influence in the new territory was also stronger. He had become a political titan. Respected and influential as a statesman, he was involved in peace treaties with the Indians. He oversaw the dispersal of lands and attempted to keep the white settlers off Indian lands. He was carving out his own indelible mark in history. Progressive in his thinking, he was able to convince his friend George Roulstone to begin publishing the first newspaper of the new territory in Rogersville. Named the *Knoxville Gazette,* its first edition was printed in November of 1791. Serving as a platform for Governor Blount, the newspaper informed citizens of Blounts orders, laws, land deals, and politics. It also advertised the current merchandise at local stores, runaway slaves, and debts owed by local residents.

From the archives at Rocky Mount, one article suggests that Mrs. Cobb and Mrs. Blount might have enjoyed the newspaper together. Each woman busied themselves preparing meals and making items for their families. Because Mrs. Cobb was aware of Molsey's "reluctance to come to the frontier because of its danger and sparseness," a newspaper advertising the latest goods would "reassure her that the frontier was not nearly as sparse as she might think."

Also of interest was the appointment of Willie, (pronounced *Why lee*) as William's new personal secretary. Willie, his half brother and nineteen years his junior, took over much of William's personal correspondence. He had completed his studies in law, and the frontier seemed perfect for someone looking for guidance and a career. William also required a confidant on his trek to the frontier. The relationship of William and Willie took on the characteristics father to son, rather than a relationship between two brothers. As common as nepotism is today, it was even more common in colonial times.

Unmarried and twenty-three years old, Willie traveled with his brother's family to the Cobbs' in December of 1791. The youngest of the Blount brothers, he had grown up at Blount Hall. Educated and capable, he remained Blount's personal secretary throughout his life in the new territory, filling in for another of William's personal secretaries, Daniel Smith. Secretary Daniel Smith had been the acting governor in William's absence, staying temporarily with the Cobbs while conducting territorial business for his boss. He also authored of the extensive manuscript *The Blount Journal 1790–1796*.

As spring cued the redbuds and the mountain laurel, Molsey and her family prepared to leave Cobbs' Rocky Mount. After three solid months of living within an overcrowded house, sharing daily squabbles and concerns, laughing through tall tales and stories of the frontier, she was ready to move on to another part of the wilderness, a town smaller than Jonesborough or Piney Flats. The hospitable Cobbs were probably just as ready for their guests to leave. Three months was a long time to give up one's privacy to a family brimming with children and the daily political and business transactions of two statesmen. The new town Knoxville beckoned Molsey's husband to more possibilities and solutions, even as it beckoned Molsey to more liabilities and problems.

11

September 1792—Knoxville, Territory South of the River Ohio

Willie knew well enough to stay out of the bedchamber. Molsey's groans and panting spurred him along as he hustled past the small wooden door, tripping on an old shoe and nearly colliding with the oak table. He had to find his brother! Leaning on the log doorway, he caught his breath and hollered for William. Molsey continued protesting the imminent birth of her child. Her heavy groaning clung to Willie's anxiety like a beached keelboat to a shallow shore.

Molsey gripped the side of her rope bed, knuckles white, while Hagar wiped her mistress's forehead. This birth was different. Gone was the comfort of a birthing chair and the elegant mattress, or even the closeness of a doctor if needed. She didn't even have her mother's hand to hold. At least Hagar was here. Molsey grabbed onto Hagar's old wrinkled hand, waiting for the next wave of pain. Her water had broken about an hour ago, and now the agony of labor began relentlessly pulling her into another groan, another cry.

In the fog of her mind, Molsey had heard Willie's calling, but her William still wasn't here. Hagar brought her focus back to the birth, patting her mistress's hand as she reached for another cloth. The bowl of water was ready. The cord to tie off the blood flow was ready, and the child was ready.

With every last ounce of breath she could muster, Molsey grimaced and pushed, then pushed some more. Hagar prodded her to push one last time. A tiny head announced the imminent birth. Suddenly, around the corner came another cry.

William, clopping into the cabin, feverishly bellowed, "I'm home! I'm here. Molsey, I'm here!" Then her little baby girl was there too. William deliberately but haltingly approached the bed. Amazement and wonder consumed him. He awkwardly sat on the chair beside his wife. Tears of relief and joy crept from the corner of Molsey's eyes. William reached for a cloth, bathing her cheeks and forehead, and pronounced, "It's a girl, Molsey, a girl—another little girl."

Hagar began to clean up the newborn, wrapping her in a soft swaddling blanket. Bringing the baby to Molsey, she handed the child first to her father. William's features melted from a strong, guarded expression to one of gentle acceptance and pride. He smiled, gently placing the babe in Molsey's arms, and then stood to leave. She did not expect him to linger after the birth. She had heard of the horrendous problems he was having with the Indians. Squeezing her hand, he bent over, kissing the babe and her mother.

"I'll be back as soon as I can," he whispered and was gone.

Hagar continued to clean up the room. She disposed of the soiled sheets and clothing and brought the cradle closer to the bed. Molsey was exhausted and preferred being alone. Delighting in the newborn's curly hair and soft mewling, she curled her arms around the baby girl.

Instinctively the babe sought out the warm breast, nuzzling and blindly finding contentment. Molsey sighed and relaxed, her body remembering that warm wonderful feeling of nursing her child. As the infant suckled, her remembering turned to thoughts of another child, another home, another change.

She recalled the uncomfortable jostling of the carriage ride to this place her husband called Knoxville. Though the weather had warmed, the leaves had been unwilling to cooperate with the parade. They had traveled though the unsettled, wild, and dangerous woods to the newly finished log cabin that was now their home. She looked around at the cramped, rugged surroundings of the small bedchamber. The tiny window barely let any light in the room. She turned her head, hair matted and sweaty, toward the door. She noticed how dark and gloomy the whole cabin was. It reminded her of all she had given up—the comfort and ease of living in the refinement and culture of a North Carolina plantation home. And now she was faced with the threat of Indians.

A 1958 photo of Rocky Mount, prior to its restoration. Molsey and three of her young children stayed here for three months during the winter of 1791–1792. The Cobbs' hospitality allowed the Blounts time to plan the building of the Blount Mansion in early 1792. Molsey and family were welcomed for several months. Willie Blount was also staying with the Cobbs. Courtesy of Rocky Mount Museum.

William had spent most of last year working on ways to prevent continued bloodshed between the whites, the Creeks, the Chickamaugas, the Chickasaws, and the Cherokees. She remembered his trip south for the signing of the Treaty of Holston. It had been his first attempt to seriously bring peace to the settlers and local tribes. She was proud of his efforts to settle the territorial claims of the Cherokee. He had formulated a plan to provide for the mutual exchange of prisoners, and he placed the Cherokee under the protection of the United States. But now William was busy again. Lately, the terms of the treaty were being challenged by everyone involved.

She pondered the promise of her husband for a better home. The cabin, built close to James White's fort, provided a sense of safety, but she yearned for a larger home for her family. Her children—Billy, Richard, and the year-old Jacob—needed their own room. Now with the newborn, she and William would need more room too, even Willie. Where would they put him? He didn't complain about sleeping on the floor of the cabin, but in the new house, William would have to etch out a place for his brother to live.

William had found land for the new house while he was here last year. Preparations for the construction of their stylish new house had been in place before she had left the Cobbs. Molsey appreciated all the Cobbs had done for her family, but now she was on her own. The safety of living close to White's fort brought her close to the chatter of frontier men, soldiers, and settlers, but she rarely heard the voice of a woman. William has busy working to change that. He focused on bringing in more residents, businesses, and taverns to the untested town of Knoxville.

Her children's silly giggles distracted her musings. She smiled tiredly as she heard their shuffles and footsteps approaching her bed. Resting on one arm and holding the newborn, she greeted Billy and Richard as they rushed to see their new little sister. Little Jacob teetered on his way to his mother, his little hand held by Venice. As all three children leaned on the bed, Molsey beamed while looking at their sweet faces. Realizing both their innocence and vulnerability, she whispered what every mother prays, "God, help me keep these children safe. Help me show them how much they are loved." Once again, Molsey was left alone to ponder life and her children's safety.

Little Barbara Blount was born on September 16, 1792, in the fledging town of Knoxville. Her birth was not attended by Mrs. Grainger, for she had remained in Greenville after the Blounts left in October of 1791. Most likely, Hagar stepped in as midwife, once more assisting Molsey with the birth of her eighth child. Without the availability of physicians, giving birth was risky for the thirty-one-year-old mother.

In correspondence dated December 12, 1792, between their family friend Hugh Williamson and John Gray Blount, Barbara's birth is noted. "You have heard I suppose the (that) Mrs. Blount has lately 2 Months ago brought a little girl, by much the finest she has ever had, it distances the others out of Sight. Such are the Benefits of good Air & wild Game." Mr. Williamson's reasoning as to what could identify the "finest" in babies was obviously lacking, but certainly the baby was healthy and welcome.

The healthy newborn was named for William's mother, Barbara. The cabin she was born in rested on a knoll near White's Fort above the Holston River. This knoll became known as Barbara's Hill or Barbary Hill. The exact location of this knoll is disputed by historians. Logically, the log home had been built near the fort for protection from the Indians and most likely on a hill. Alice Keith in volume 2 of the *John Gray Blount Papers* positions the log home "below College Hill, and between it and the river."

Governor Blount had arrived and established the town of Knoxville in 1791. He had selected an area near White's Fort between two creeks—the First Creek and the Second Creek—for his permanent capital. Blount had traveled extensively, carefully seeking a place to establish his capital for the new territory. Through late 1791 and early 1792, he had arranged for a temporary home for his family, a small log home. The selection for his capital was determined by its access to the Holston River, the protection of White's Fort, and because the Cherokee had not agreed with his first selection, which was further north in the Kingston region, a place called Emory's Town.

Soon after selecting the location for his new capital, he named it Knoxville after Henry Knox, his immediate supervisor in Washington, DC. Lots were sold to prospective settlers, including Blount. Walter Durham notes in *Before Tennessee: The Southwest Territory, 1790–1796* that Blount also began constructing "the first two-story frame house in the Territory, and one of the first west of the Blue Ridge Mountains." He was intent on building a home and a place of government that would impress all who came to Knoxville, especially Molsey. In January of 1792, he ordered glass for his mansion, a luxury in any frontier home. He wrote his friend John Sevier, asking for his help with the shipment of a glass from Richmond. Obviously, Molsey was aware that her new mansion was meant to be similar to the home she had left behind.

However, the home she first arrived at was not luxurious. Molsey and her three sons lived in the log cabin from March of 1792 until the mansion was completed sometime in late 1792 or early 1793. Three months pregnant, she would have spent many anxious moments corralling her children as they played and keeping them as close to her as she could. At the same time, she had to manage setting up the new household, supervising the domestic slaves as they carried out her needs and orders. Other slaves were busy clearing land, planting gardens and crops, and constructing the new "White House."

In early 1792, Knoxville was a wilderness, except for an area surrounding White's Fort that had been cleared. The abundance of turkey, deer, rabbit, bear, cougar, quail, and fish supplied Molsey's kitchen with food enough for her family and the slaves. The new town was in direct conflict with Native American traditions of the Cherokee, Chickasaw, Creek, and Chickamauga tribes. The Indians had no concept of owning land or selling land for monetary profit. This inerrant difference in custom led to unpredictable and unrelenting conflicts. The constant threat of

Indian attacks or the burning of frontier homes was always on the Blounts' minds.

It wasn't long after Molsey and her three boys arrived in Knoxville that the Indian attacks grew into a greater threat. In April and May of 1792, Blount attempted to appease the Indians, but fraudulent trading practices with them, murders, attacks, and ambushes on both sides undermined his efforts, and months of violence followed. Blount had intended to take Molsey, who was approximately five months pregnant, with him to visit the Cherokees in the town of Coyatee, planning to distribute gifts among the Indians. However, Historian Alice Keith notes a change. In the *John Gray Blount Papers, Volume 2* it is revealed that "the killing of three whites on the Cumberland Road, induced him to postpone his appearance." In mid-1792, it seemed Blount did not have a clear understanding of the Indian situation. Inviting his pregnant wife to accompany him into Indian territory spoke of a lack of common sense, or at least thoughtlessness, on his part.

Treaty of Holston Memorial in Volunteer Landing Park in downtown Knoxville.

Image of William Blount on Holston Memorial, located on the banks of Tennessee River, where the treaty was signed. In 1792, the river was named the Holston River.

Blount found himself pulled in two directions. Indian affairs were critical, needing an immediate solution, but the settlement of Knoxville was also important. With his main interest in land, he purchased 220 acres with James White early on at Second Creek. He asked his friend George Roulstone to bring his printing press to the frontier and advertise the new location. Roulstone began printing his newspaper *The Knoxville Gazette* from Rogersville.

Announcing the recent founding of Knoxville, Roulstone stated in his paper:

> It is situate on the north bank of the Holston, on a beautiful eminence, twenty-six miles from the mouth where it empties into the great river Tennessee, and four below the mouth of French Broad, North latitude 35 42"; distant from Philadelphia 638, from Baltimore, 543, and from Richmond 458 miles, (to each of which there is a good waggon road;) from the Beloved Town of Chota of the Cherokees, 25 miles, and but little more from sundry other of their towns on the (Little) Tennessee, and from Nashville, nearly east, 205 miles.

It wasn't long before new settlers ventured to Knoxville. More of a land speculator than a city builder, Blount frequently traveled between the future Nashville area, named Mero, and Knoxville. In fact, Blount was never actually a permanent resident of Knoxville. Though he built a mansion there, he continued traveling throughout the new territory and North Carolina, staying home only for brief intervals between his sojourns. Molsey also would not live permanently in Knoxville. She frequently traveled back to North Carolina to escape the dangers of an Indian attack or to visit family.

The Knoxville Gazette was very thorough in its coverage of Indian problems. In the first edition printed in Rogersville on November 1791, one reads:

> On Wednesday evening last Mr. James Kilpatric was killed by a party of Indians on Poor Valley Creek, about 17 miles from Hawkins Courthouse and 3 miles from the main Kentucky road. Mr. Kilpatric had gone out to drive up his cattle, and was not more than 400 yards from his house when the Indians fired on him; they instantly made off without attempting to scalp him.

Soon Knoxville had United States troops situated at the fort, located at the current corner of Gay and Main Streets, to protect settlers.

Horse stealing was another problem. Roulstone records in November of 1791:

> Stolen out of Mr. Joseph Rogers's pasture at Rogersville on Tuesday night, the 18th instant, a likely dark bay horse, fiftenne hands high, a star in his forehead, blind of the left eye, branded on the near shoulder I T, and on the near buttocks H O Y. Whoever will take up said horse, and deliver him to Mr. Rogers, shall receive five dollars reward.

Not only did Indians steal horses, but white settlers were also guilty of stealing them from the Indians.

Even with the ongoing problems with the Indians, Blount remained faithful to his mercantile interests and his deep-seated need to earn more money. His move into the Knoxville area provided him the opportunity to invest in the enlargement of a small ironworks factory, the King Ironworks. As Masterson puts it, Blount held an event that "celebrated for two days with games, races, wrestling, and various feats of strength rewarded by prizes bestowed by the governor himself." Molsey was part of this celebration too. Blount had arranged for his wife to christen the new furnace, which was made for ore and charcoal. The furnace was christened for Blount's mother and perhaps his new daughter. On a raised platform, Molsey hammered a bottle of rum on the furnace, announcing its name as the Barbara.

The construction of the Blount Mansion called for thorough planning and organization in relation to the details of the kitchen, bedchambers for the children, furnishings, and household items. Molsey most certainly would have shared in a large part of that planning. While Blount managed the area that would be his office, the details of creating a functioning life on the frontier would have fallen on Molsey's shoulders. When William and Molsey moved into the mansion, they needed to provide sleeping rooms for Willie, Billy (eight), Richard (four), Jacob (one), and Barbara, who was only a few months old. The original mansion included two rooms, a hall, and a parlor, with the upstairs loft or attic reached by a steep staircase or ladder. With the children situated upstairs, Molsey and William lived in cramped quarters in comparison with today's standards for privacy and space. The assumption is that the couple slept in the parlor with the young children while Willie, Billy, and Richard were upstairs until such time that other rooms could be added.

Blount Mansion: Current front of Mansion, the original two-story structure.

Today, Blount Mansion's front door faces Hill Avenue. When initially constructed, the mansion's front door faced the river with a small porch beside it. William had built a detached kitchen and office, along with a slave quarters in front of the original porch.

There are no remains of a barn or barnyard on the property. This suggests that Molsey didn't keep her many and much-beloved horses nearby. All through her life in North Carolina, horses had been an important aspect of her daily activities. She enjoyed attending horse races, traveling about in a carriage pulled by her matching dappled grays, and buying and selling horses. Once her family was living in Knoxville, it appears that horses were no longer a part of her life, which raises the question, How did the Blounts travel? Where were their horses?

There are two possible answers to those questions. The Blounts owned acreage near the current University of Tennessee campus, which was their "farm." Since it was important to remain close to the fort for safety, the distant farm provided necessary crops, timber, and gardens. Perhaps their horses were kept at the farm, or perhaps the Blounts had use of horses owned by their friend John Chisholm. Chisholm owned the lot located behind the Blount mansion, where he built the Chisholm Tavern. As a bustling town where travelers would come to relax and stay, it would have included a stable, capable of providing the Blounts with horses when needed.

New to Knoxville, Molsey's immediate job was to keep her family warm, fed, clothed, and comfortable. She oversaw the organization of the household, the gathering of food, and the ordering of clothing and materials for her family and slaves. She was in charge of all the day-to-day functions necessary to maintain two households—the log cabin and the future mansion. The planting of a garden for vegetables was an immediate concern in order to provide enough food for the Blounts during their first winter. Dried fruits and vegetables would have been shipped to the governor's house, along with seeds, plantings, and fruit trees.

When William left North Carolina in 1790, the census indicated that he owned thirty slaves. It is unclear how many of those slaves the Blounts brought with them in their move to the mountains. The Blounts had always treated their slaves well. William's personal slave, Jack, lacked for nothing. Blount was determined that his slaves reflect his own sense of propriety and well-being. He never wanted to be embarrassed by the condition, dress, or manners of his slaves.

A 1797 inventory of the household indicates that the Blounts owned twenty-seven slaves. William was always aware of the necessity of slaves on his plantations. In his Knoxville residences, slaves ensured his future economic well-being. While preparations were being made in the construction of the mansion, slaves played a large part in the labor. Formerly plantation slaves, their duties had changed. The Southwest Territory was not flat like North Carolina. Plantations did not exist in the Knoxville area. There were no slaves in tobacco, rice, or cotton fields. Therefore, the Blount slaves would have cultivated specific skills that Blount could utilize in building his homes, clearing his lands, working in the nail factory, and cultivating the red earth. Molsey would have had several domestic slaves working within the two homes, preparing meals and caring for the children.

Information from Blount Mansion files clearly names Molsey's slaves. Hagar appears throughout all the Blount history. When Molsey's father died, she inherited "little Hagar," who later traveled with her to the territory. Hagar's importance in Molsey's life cannot be understated.

Hagar was companion and nurse to Molsey before she was married, eventually assuming the role of nurse and midwife in her adult years. As noted in the *Blount Mansion Interpreter's Manual*, her daily responsibilities would have included "bathing and dressing [Molsey and the children], preparing the fires, [and] warming the bed with the bedwarmer." Without Molsey's mother in residence at the cabin or mansion, Hagar would have assisted on her own with the birth of Barbara.

Other known slaves close to Molsey were Sall and Cupid. The *Blount Mansion Interpreter's Manual* informs us of other jobs Sall and Cupid performed within the Blount household. This couple and their children appear in Blount history as attending to "public and semi-public areas." Sall was most likely Molsey's cook, an extremely important job in the transition from North Carolina.

Cupid is reported as an assistant to Blount's personal slave, Jack, assisting him with "serving the meals, tending to guests, and moving the furniture." These slaves remained with the Blount family until after Molsey died.

Toward the end on 1792, Blount showed no interest in the slave trade in the Southwest Territory, only in taxing the residents of the lands west of the mountains. *The Blount Papers* indicate on November 10, 1792, that he authorized the county courts to levy a tax. The tax was "for repairing or building Courthouses, prisons and stocks in the said counties respectively, to pay Jurors to the Superior courts and defray the contingent charges of the said counties." Even with this tax, Knoxville did not immediately construct a jail. Blount struggled to bring income to the frontier. The tax amounted to income from lands and polls. The counties "shall not extend to levying a tax, in any one year, on each poll of more than fifty cents, nor on each hundred acres of land, of more than seventeen cents."

As a member of the upper gentry, William brought to Knoxville a sense of respectability and substantial power within the government he directed. Molsey brought to Knoxville a sense of dignity and restraint. Janice McKenny described her in *Women of the Constitution: Wives of the Signers* as "a gentle, lovable woman…" Ramsey went on to describe her as "…an accomplished lady, and she did much to soften and refine the manners of the first inhabitants of Knoxville."

In looking back, it's not hard to see that this journey into the wilderness called for a strong woman. As such, we discover a combination of strengths and complications in Molsey. She was refined and reluctant, arriving pregnant, frightened, and disoriented as a result of her husband's political and economic ambitions, but she was determined to overcome whatever hardships she faced.

The strength and resolve needed to forge a home, a life, and the well-being for her family is unquestionable. What remains were the variables in the environment she encountered when she traveled to the frontier. How was she able to manage maintaining manners, civility, fashion, demeanor, and a social code in the face of Indian attacks, buckskin leggings and jackets, and narrow dirt paths instead of brick pathways? Wilderness culture was unrefined, defined by natural elements and the uncomfortable. Molsey did a remarkable job in establishing a home for her family, a home far away from her two children and the life she had known in North Carolina.

Nancy and Louisa had remained in North Carolina, as did Molsey's mother. To Molsey, it must have seemed a lifetime away—if not a country away. Her homeland probably frequently beckoned to her. I'm certain she yearned to see her older girls and her mother. Would she ever return? How could this place ever be her real home?

Not long after arriving in late 1792, William left to settle Indian affairs, leaving Molsey with a newborn and three young children. She understood this to be her new home and knew she had to find a way to settle in Knoxville as she watched the building of the mansion. Yet it wasn't long before she returned to her homeland, heading east for safety and the solace of familiar surroundings and family.

12

May 1, 1794—
Somewhere near Salem, North Carolina

"How much longer? Are we there yet, Mother?" whined five-year-old Richard as he fussed and squirmed in the cramped carriage seat. His older brother, Billy, elbowed him as he tried to lean out the carriage window. The children were tired, bored, and restless after several days riding in the new carriage. Uncle John held three-year-old Jacob on his lap while Molsey bounced the curly-haired toddler Barbara on hers. Both adults remained silent as the miles slowly crept by. The flat land of eastern North Carolina slowly etched itself with hills and small mountains as they jostled along. Those growing mountains reminded Molsey of her mounting anticipation and excitement.

Almost nine months had passed since she had last seen her husband. They had parted ways in September of the previous year when his coach crested the hill on its way to Knoxville while she remained in Greenville. It seemed they had been forever saying good-bye all through their fifteen years of marriage. Once back in Knoxville, perhaps they would be able to find a way to remain closer, to stay together. He had written to her from Knoxville of new Indian problems, old land warrants, and little emotion. Her letters to him had been lost in the mail or hidden beneath piles of government documents.

The road sign they passed indicated only five miles to Salem, the town that promised new beginnings and her husband's warm, wonderful smile. William had instructed John to meet him in Salem, North Carolina. His half brother Sharpe would also be

145

there. The town had been established decades ago by the Moravian Church and its members. Her brothers-in-law had been told to go to the town's center, near the Single Brothers' House. This trade town was an excellent choice for them to meet up at, with its local tavern and bakery near the town square. The carriage slowed, approaching their destination. The mixture of anxiety and joy made Molsey's stomach flip-flop. Placing Barbara on the floorboard between the seats, she strained to look out window, blocked by her sons' heads.

As the horses came to a stop, she saw three men gathered together outside the tavern. Recognizing his hat and graying hair, she smiled instantly, trying to wave above the children. Finally, there he was at the carriage. John reached to open the door, and out tumbled three giggling and excited boys. Billy threw his arms around his father's waist as Richard and Jacob teetered about his legs. John exited next, turning to help Molsey out of the carriage.

William, entwined with children, leaned toward her. Molsey fell into his arms. At last, the familiar comfort of her husband. She didn't want to move but was forced to as Billy insisted on showing his father the latest book he was reading, Richard thrust his new toy in his father's face, and Jacob shook his ragged, much-loved stuffed dog up beside it. The noise was a wonderful cacophony of warm welcome.

That evening, the reunited family chattered over a meal of venison and vegetables, with cheese and wine for the adults. Each child incessantly regaled their father with all they had to tell. William listened patiently, his eyes often glancing at Molsey. John sat back, smiling as he watched the reunion, reflecting on his own family back in North Carolina. Sharpe spoke of Blount Hall and the latest news from home. It wasn't long before the tired and road-weary children were put to bed, leaving William, Molsey, John, and Sharpe talking in the candlelit great room of the tavern. It felt so good to finally touch his hand, to lean against him and just listen to his voice, so warm and sure. The three brothers were completely engrossed in business talk and land matters. Molsey

146

excused herself, heading off to check on the children before going to bed.

When she awoke at dawn the next morning, she noticed William had already risen. She quickly donned her clothing and hurried to the great hall, catching sight of Richard sitting on his father's knee, eating an apple while John urgently discussed legal matters. Making a quick count of her children, she noted that Billy was outside playing with a dog while both little Jacob and Barbara were still abed, sleeping. She settled quietly beside William, squeezing his hand. However, she had no sooner become comfortable before the cry of her youngest arose from upstairs. Where was Hagar? She stood up, frowning slightly as she headed outside to search for her slave. Where was Hagar when she should be getting the children dressed and fed? From behind the quarters back of the tavern, Hagar hurried toward Molsey, all the while fastening her apron, determined to reach her before she called her again.

After breakfast, their carriage was readied, the children delighted to be leaving with their father. William left his brother John with several last-minute instructions as John eagerly prepared to head east. With a handshake and pat on the shoulder, William parted from his brother. John smiled and nodded his acknowledgement, turning to leave. As John's carriage began its way homeward, the brothers waved amiably to each other. The Blount children were just as ready to leave for home too.

As everyone scrambled into the carriage, Molsey settled next to William, ready and eager to begin her journey back to the frontier. William had reassured her that it was safer now. When she had left in May of 1793, the Creeks and Cherokees had become unpredictable. Some of the tribes were settling treaties with William, but others were still burning homes, scalping, and killing settlers. The white settlers weren't any help in keeping the peace either. Knoxville had been threatened and the frontier aflame. She had wanted nothing more than to leave and return to North Carolina. Now she was returning with four of her children to the

147

new mansion they had built above the Holston River. How long would she have to stay this time?

⟶ formatting flourish ⟵

In May of 1794, Molsey Blount repeated the long journey from Greenville, North Carolina, to the frontier, just as she had done in October of 1791. Though not staying with the Cobbs at Rocky Mount, the journey mimicked the discomforts of the long carriage ride over the Appalachian Mountains. Having left Blount Mansion in late May of 1793, she and her children had stayed with her mother for almost a year, probably in their former Greenville home. Away from the frontier town and the daily threat of Indian attacks for a year, she had been able to visit with her family, live in comfort, and surround herself with friends and well-wishers.

Separations were common in the Blount marriage. This most recent separation had heralded a nine-month absence from each other before their next reunion, and it would not be the last. They had visited briefly in North Carolina, but William returned to Knoxville without her. Molsey's thoughts and feelings about returning to the wilderness are not captured in history. As a matter of conjecture, she would have probably had some reservations about leaving the safety, comfort, and luxury of North Caroline again for the bare-bones village of Knoxville.

William's efforts to build Knoxville into the capital of the territory were slowly taking shape. By late 1792, the town had a courthouse located near the residence of Esquire Rogers. A jail, made of logs, was being constructed at the current corner of Main and Gay streets, measuring fourteen feet by fourteen feet. A few small log homes dotted the young town of Knoxville, along with a barracks that stood on the current lot of Blount Mansion. Land had been cleared around the barracks, a two-story building overlooking the Holston River. By 1794, the small town had attracted more settlers, holding tenaciously to recurrent and ever-changing relationships with the Cherokee, the Creek, and the Chickamauga Indian tribes.

Molsey had to be reflecting on what she was once again leaving behind. Her two oldest children, Nancy and Louisa, would have been foremost on her mind. Also, she left her mother once more and would not see her for another year or so. Adding to her feelings of loss, would be her favorite horses. By now, William had ordered the sale of many of them; any particular horse that had survived the sale would have also remained in North Carolina since the Blounts did not keep horses at the Knoxville mansion.

The children were a year older. Barbara, not quite two years old, and Jacob, almost three years old, would not have remembered their frontier mansion, whereas Richard, then five, and William, almost ten, would recall their life in Knoxville. Excited and delighted with this new adventure, the two older boys would have chattered throughout the long journey home, especially now that they had their father's company.

As eager as William was to have his family with him again, he was also well aware of the perils and problems they still faced in Knoxville. He had spent the last part of 1793 and early 1794 embroiled in Indian matters, guiding the building of forts to protect white settlers, enlarging militia forces, attempting to stop white incursions into Indian lands, and juggling his private land transactions. Problems with Sevier and White added to his struggles. On a more personal note, he was lonely and missed his family.

Therefore, Blount left Knoxville in late April to meet up with his family and his brother John Gray Blount in the Moravian town of Salem. In the late eighteenth century, this religious settlement was a thriving, hardworking community committed to the Moravian Church. No one owned land in Salem. Instead, residents leased land from the church and submitted to the church's authority. Blount probably chose this town as a place to meet because of its reputation as a trade town. The Moravians were famous for their fine furniture, pottery, delicious food, and

149

their production of metal objects, distilled goods, and leather items. The neat, well-organized town was built around a central square that offered housing to single men in the Single Brothers' House and for single women in the nearby Single Sisters' House. Salem seemed the perfect place to meet his errant family and his brothers John and Sharpe.

Most historians agree that Willie remained in Knoxville whenever William traveled. Standing in for William during his absence, Willie supervised government matters and oversaw the upkeep of the mansion and the supervision of the Blount slaves, missing out on visiting with his other brother John Gray. John was asked by William to escort Molsey, the children, and her slaves on their journey to Salem from Greenville.

He also had another agenda for meeting up with his brother. In reading the *John Gray Blount Letters* for this time period, it is obvious that John and William's business matters were extremely important. A flurry of letters between the brothers prior to this meeting indicates a sense of urgency and accomplishment. They would have discussed a myriad of business concerns regarding their holdings on the Tar River, their shipping business, and their interests in the production of tar, turpentine, lumber, and naval stores. The other major topic of interest was land.

Previously, John had been involved in a land scheme to secure four million acres of North Carolina land that would yield another five hundred thousand acres for the Blount brothers. He was also in the process of organizing several land surveys that would add even more to the Blounts' steadily growing, colossal amount of acreage. Their face-to-face conversations in Salem would have been intense and zealous. Masterson referenced their land speculation as "… the overwhelming trend was accretion in the Eastern area, in Mero, and even on the Mississippi."

Whether Molsey was aware of the huge amounts of land the Blount brothers commandeered can only be guessed at. The couple had much to catch up on regarding their family and their latest separation. The long ride over the mountains back to

Knoxville would have provided them with hours to converse, absorbing all the details that letters couldn't contain.

While William had been consumed by the politics of Knoxville and the family businesses, Molsey's year away from the Blount Mansion had been full of domestic changes, family concerns, and the day-to-day responsibilities of managing the Greenville plantation without her husband. Her autonomy and freedom of choice brought out further strengths within her personality.

Returning to the fall of 1792, we recall how Molsey had given birth to Barbara, moved into the new mansion, and adjusted to her first winter in Knoxville, all within a few months. Her fondness for her new home dwindled with each reported atrocity committed by belligerent white settlers or offended Indians. Both she and William became increasingly uncomfortable with menacing tribes so close to their children and their home. Willie and Molsey, in agreement with William, planned a trip to North Carolina for safety, taking the children with them.

William also began to consider leaving Knoxville. His three-year appointment as territorial Governor was scheduled to expire in 1794. He needed to return to Philadelphia. Besides, Henry Knox had requested he journey to the US capital with delegates from the Cherokee and Chickamauga tribes. So it was decided. The Blounts would leave the frontier for a brief time, hopefully in May of 1793. In a congenial parting gesture as governor, Blount held a going-away reception, complete with a formal address to the citizens of Knoxville. Delayed a bit, he headed for Philadelphia while Molsey headed home on June 7, 1793.

Awaiting Molsey's arrival in Hillsborough, North Carolina, was her brother-in-law Thomas. He had gone to meet her carriage in late May, but she and the children did not arrive. In the *John Gray Blount Papers,* Thomas notes, "...I waited 20 Days in expectation of Seeing Molsey but was so completely disappointed that I did not even hear of her—Sharpe is gone to Salem where he will wait for her until the 12th Instant." The Blount carriages had been delayed due to rains, rutty roads, and frequent stops to visit with friends and political allies. William encouraged his newspaper friend, Roulstone, to ride with him to Jonesboro, and Masterson shares that "…Sevier later joined for a ten mile ride and long, confidential talk."

Troubles pursued the carriages as the family approached the mountain passes. Blount heard news that back in Knoxville, the slaughter of a prominent Indian and his family had the area aflame with Cherokee retaliation. William was tempted to return to Knoxville but continued to Virginia, parting with Molsey and the children on June 20, 1793. As noted in the *Correspondence of William Blount*, the Governor noted on June 17, 1793, "I shall pass the mountain with Mrs. Blount who with her party has thus for arrived safe… the day after tomorrow and the next day leave her and turn off for the Richmond from whence I shall take the stage." It would be months and months before the family would be together again.

Molsey and her children continued on their way to the Greenville plantation, ultimately reuniting with her mother in late June or early July. Among familiar faces and routines, she quickly assumed her former position, managing the domestic slaves and supervising the plantation. Again, the *John Gray Blount Papers, Volume 2* reveal a concern of William. He often asked his brothers to check on Molsey: "I depend on you to provide for her Household and to give her your advice in all Cases."

Since the postal routes were more efficient in North Carolina than they were in the Knoxville area, she heard by letter that William was once again ill. He had suffered reoccurring bouts of malaria while in Richmond and Alexandria, Virginia, impeding his journey to Philadelphia. Eventually he arrived at the capital, still recovering from the fever.

Molsey was also exposed to debilitating diseases. Yellow fever was raging through the East Coast in the summer of 1793, creating worries and concerns for her. By September, one of her children was quite sick.

Living in Tarborough with her uncle Thomas and her aunt Ann, Louisa fell critically ill, most likely with yellow fever. Thomas, himself also ill with malaria, wrote to his brother John, revealing the seriousness of the fever, "Mary (Louisa) is yet alive contrary to expectation of us all & a change that has taken place this Morning affords us some hope that she will recover…Nancy & Billy Orr are the only well persons in the family—My Sister is fatigued almost to death & complains heavily but Keeps up—I dread the consequences to her." Molsey visited Tarborough during this illness yet is not reported to be either ill or well.

All was not well with Molsey's mother either. Though not ill, she was dealing with legal problems that William struggled to solve for her from a distance. As her protector, he was involved in a lawsuit originating in Wilmington, the Grainger homeland, and worried about the outcome of this lawsuit and its effect on his own wealth. Alice Keith supplies the details in volume 2 of the *John Gray Blount Papers*. Apparently, William had hired a lawyer, Alfred Moore, to defend her, who "I have paid a handsome Fee in Guineas, five or ten I forget which." Mrs. Grainger appeared to have complicated the matter. William tells his brother John to make sure "…that she does not write or verbally acknowledge or say what may be improper on the Occasion…" Her son-in-law viewed success in this lawsuit as another supplement to his voracious appetite for more income. "It is an important Suit for whatever is saved to Mrs. Grainger is saved to me."

In the same letter, William continued with discussions of family matters. Molsey had decided to stay in North Carolina with the children for the winter of 1793–1794. The instability of the Indian predicament had led the family to consider staying permanently in North Carolina.

William wrote to John on September 19, 1793, as recorded in the *Blount Papers*, "I rejoice much that She is off the Frontiers and a respectable Distance from the *Jacobian* Part of the Cherokee & Creek Nation." He returned to Knoxville in the fall of 1793 while Molsey remained safely in North Carolina.

The safety provided for Molsey and her children continued through the generous acts of her husband's brothers. Thomas was directed to sell off her horses, something that would have been difficult for her. Although she had always been surrounded by horses, she surely must have realized the necessity of the sale. Raising children was expensive, and William was not there to sort through those expenses.

Thomas wrote to John telling him that he needed more money to care for Nancy and Louisa, who remained with him in Tarborough even after their mother had returned to North Carolina. He had enrolled them in a six-week dancing program with the dancing master Roselle but didn't have enough money to pay for the lessons, which would begin in December of 1793. There is no response recorded in history by Molsey about this dilemma. Thomas asked his brother, "at a Dollar P Day each— Will you be able & willing at that time to spare 80 or 90 Dollars to pay Mr. Roselle?" as detailed by Alice Keith.

Molsey's time back in North Carolina was also laced with joyous occasions. In early September, Nancy, the first wife of Jacob Blount, gave birth to their first child. Though Jacob and Nancy lived north of Greenville in Edenton, Molsey had her carriage and pair of matching horses. This allowed her the freedom to visit them, probably taking along her younger children to proudly show off to all the relatives. Other nieces and nephews made their appearance while Molsey was visiting North Carolina.

Weddings were also occasions of celebration. Molsey was able to attend two family weddings in February of 1794. Reading Blount, eight years younger than William, wed Lucy Harvey, the sister to John Gray Blount's wife, Mary. Sharpe Blount, the youngest Blount brother, married Penelope Little.

As the spring of 1794 approached, Molsey realized it was time to return to the frontier. William wrote her of his plans to meet her in May somewhere in the middle of North Carolina. Postal communications were slowly improving. William had asked Congress to build a post office at William Cobbs and eventually another one down the Holston River at Knoxville. Paul Phillips notes in "Never a Safe Road" (*Journal of East Tennessee History* 1990), initially, mail was delivered by private means via the old Wilderness Road out of Abingdon, Virginia, by a "trusted family member, traveling merchant, itinerant preacher, military man, Indian agent or express rider." Mail delivery had improved by 1794, ensuring steady delivery between William, his brothers, and Molsey.

In late March, William directed Molsey and his brother John to meet him in Salem, North Carolina. Once again, Molsey gathered her belongings, children, and slaves, along with her courage, to return to Knoxville. Strangely, she again left her two oldest daughters behind with Thomas and his sister Ann. Thomas was busy in Philadelphia convincing the government of their need for a lighthouse on the barrier islands of North Carolina and wasn't at home when Molsey left. John Gray and Sharpe agreed to chaperone Molsey and the children, meeting up William in Salem. Land deals needed the brothers' attention, and Molsey and the children needed an escort. For now, she only wanted to be with her husband again—one more coupling, one more parting.

13

Early Summer 1795—Knoxville, Territory South of the River Ohio

Molsey sucked in a soft, silent, long deep breath. She nervously straightened a stray curl about her ear with a slender finger, self-consciously standing straight as she could, stretching to add another inch or two to her height. Hagar whispered to her that the Indians were here, approaching from the river. She took another deep breath, fighting to steady every fiber of her being. She voiced the question to herself, "Why in the world did I invite them to my home?" William had thought it was about time she met several of the friendly Cherokee chiefs. He had reassured her that her hospitality would be appreciated, that the Indians would view it as evidence he was sincere in his offer of friendship to them. So here she was, waiting for such foreign dignitaries as she could never have imagined.

She peered around the gray linen curtain, peeking out the window, hoping they couldn't see her. And there they were. Three Cherokee chieftains advanced to her front porch. Their choppy words to each other sounded foreign and strange as she watched the sunlight bounce off their silver gorgets and earrings. They looked so stern and formidable, half their faces painted red. She told herself they wouldn't be long in the mansion since William planned to talk with them in his office. But for now, here they were, on her front porch.

Cupid opened the door, letting them in. They came in slowly, cautiously, looking around at the windows, the rugs, the hallway chairs. Molsey paused, holding back, then drew one last deep breath of strength and courage before stepping into the hall, bringing herself abruptly face-to-face with three Cherokee chiefs. William's interpreter, Arthur Coodey, appeared from behind them, positioning himself close to Molsey. She smiled. The chiefs nodded. The interpreter introduced Little Turkey, Black Fox, and Chuleowee.

Each party quietly sized up the other, the gears of their minds working to interpret what they had yet to understand. The Cherokee leaders purposefully ignored any direct acknowledgment of Molsey, focusing instead on Coodey's words and hands. Molsey waited as if outside herself, glancing awkwardly at their clothing. She made some mental notes. The main tribesman, Little Turkey, was slightly taller than she, his painted head and facial tattoos an indication of his authority. Was that a British coat of arms on Black Fox's gorget? The other Indian, the tallest one, smelled of smoke, bear grease, and leather. One of his strong hands grasped the feet of a dead turkey hen hanging at his side while he shifted in obvious discomfort from one foot to another. Molsey stared at the dead bird as Coodey explained that the Indians had brought her a gift.

Turning toward Hagar, who stood ready behind the parlor doorway, Molsey, for all her inward anxiety, calmly motioned her forward. Molsey then accepted the gift, taking it from the chief's hand and giving it over to her slave. Turning toward Coodey, she asked him to invite the chiefs into the parlor. She had prepared a small table of apple tarts, corn bread, bread pudding, and tea. The simple but elegantly laid table suddenly seemed out of place as she watched the Indians enter her parlor. Her senses, strung tight under the veneer of her calm, continued to focus on every little detail—their shaved heads and feathered crown patches, leather leggings, breechcloths, armbands, and linen trade shirts. How she wished William would hurry.

She recalled how William had worked his magic to comfort her, reassuring her that the Indians meant her no harm. They were only coming to Knoxville to collect a part of their tribe's annual annuity. Aware that some Indians had chosen neutrality and government payments, Molsey couldn't help but consider the recent and unpredictable attacks by some Chickamaugas and Creeks. She also remembered her manners.

With the help of her interpreter, she graciously gestured for the Indians to partake in the simple foods. She proudly stood by the well-laid table, proffering her guests gifts of food and drink. The Cherokees approached, nodding to each other and expressing their gratitude with a heavily accented "thank you." With those two unadorned words, Molsey smiled again, finally able to relax in the realization that she no longer need fear their presence.

No sooner did the insistent chains of fear fall away before William walked into the parlor, his gait assuredly confident as he added his own welcome to the Cherokee chiefs. Giggles tittered behind him from the hallway. Molsey knew what that meant—the muffled voices of her children, unable to resist peeking at the Indians in their home. Billy and Richard were away at school, but little four-year-old Jacob and Barbara, only three, just couldn't hold back. William motioned to the youngsters, permitting them to enter and see the Cherokees. Shyly they crept toward their mother, never taking their wide eyes off the Indians. With their final few steps, they sped to their mother, finding shelter behind her skirts. Little Turkey, like his companions, noted the children but said nothing.

Molsey and William, quietly smiling in pride, soon realized the dance around their mother's skirts was a distraction. Hagar appeared, taking the children in hand and shuffling them outside. With just a hint of protest, Jacob took hold of his little sister's hand and followed Hagar out of the house. The Indian delegation visibly relaxed, finishing their last bites of corn bread. William then motioned them to follow him to his office behind the mansion.

Little Turkey caught Molsey's eye as he turned to follow William. Without a word, his nod to her signaled his approval of her and her home. The two others, also silent, tread quietly and regally behind their partner, and Molsey couldn't help but consider how truly dignified they were. As they descended the front steps, she listened to their foreign chatter, underscoring her perception of their approval of Molsey's hospitality. She sighed, straightening the tablecloth and brushed aside a few crumbs.

Blount Mansion: Blount's Office at right of photo, near original Mansion.

An infant's beseeching cry rang out from the detached kitchen. Her thoughts were instantly consumed by her newest infant's need for her. Hagar and Sall would attend to the dishes and bowls on the table. For now, she wanted— no, needed—to pacify her infant girl, Eliza. Born in March, she was barely six months old, with a healthy pair of lungs. Demanding and unfashionable, Eliza's cry met Molsey as she called to Sall to bring the baby to her.

Holding her child close, the recent memory about the Indians' presence in her husband's office floated away like so much mist on a sunny morning. For now, every facet of her body and soul was consumed with this sweet little one who needed her mother. Ambling to a comfortable chair by the window, she settled down, preparing to nurse. Her smile softened as she reminisced on how

Eliza had come to be named. William and she had bantered amiably for the rights to name this child. He wanted Indiana. She wanted Eliza. Ultimately they compromised, giving her both names. At the age of thirty-four, this would be her last pregnancy and birth, this precious child, the last one to be named in the William Blount family.

～❦❦❦～

William and Molsey Blount's youngest child was born in Knoxville on March 19, 1795, a few days before her father's forty-sixth birthday. She was enthusiastically welcomed into a busy, ever-expanding family, the ninth child for Molsey and her last live birth. At that time, four other Blount children lived in the mansion, which was bursting at its seams though originally designed to accommodate the whole family. The home had been designed as a model home for genteel members of society. Billy (eleven), Richard (six), Jacob (four), and Barbara (three), all required a larger dinner table, more sleeping chambers, and space for toys and clothing.

The birth of Eliza Indiana was a time of great pride for William. In a letter to his brother John, which would have usually been filled with detailed directions and comments about their business transactions, he noted, "On the 19th Instant Molsey was delivered of a Daughter both as well as can be expected—the Child is praised for size & Beauty—The Name is doubtful Mosey says Eliza, I say Indiana to Settle the Dispute perhaps we shall take both..." William also revealed his impatience and disgust with his job as governor in the exact same letter. "...I am disgusted of the rascally Neglect of Congress & weary of the Duties of office—However this is my country under all Circumstances, a great Field is yet to open..." Blount had been at the wheel of local government for four years, steering the territory through continual hazards. The obviously growing burden of keeping his ever-expanding family safe compounded the stress he was under.

For Molsey, the daily tension of living as First Lady in a frontier wilderness remained an ongoing challenge. While Knoxville had attracted more and more settlers, the town was always on guard in relation to the Indians, even though the town's defense had proven sufficient in the past. White's Fort, the main fortress in the settlement, along with the military presence of former King's Mountain soldiers, was ever-vigilant, protecting the settlers from all Indian attacks.

The reconstructed James White Fort is in downtown Knoxville, Tennessee. When the Blounts moved to the frontier, the fort was the anchor to safety. The Blount Mansion was built near the fort.

The Indian tribes themselves were split in their loyalties toward American settlers. The various treaties and promises made by the white man, representing an ongoing and ever changing chain of authority, had to be confusing to them. The British, the French, and the Spanish had interests in the frontier during earlier years, long before Blount had arrived. The State of Franklin, under John Sevier's leadership, had also made treaties with the Indians. By 1790, that political fraction had been dissolved, pretty much negating any and all said treaties. Sorting out the myriads of treaties that had been made by these various governing powers was daunting, to say the least. Blount was often exasperated by misunderstandings and miscommunications between the whites and Indians. Molsey certainly was often privy to her husband's discussions and frustrations regarding Indian relationships in Knoxville's early history.

The Cherokee capital had moved to Unstanali, near present-day Calhoun, Georgia. The Overhill Nation lived south of Knoxville in the Indian towns of Tallassee, Chilhowie, Citico, Chestua, Toquo, Echota, Tellico, Hiwassee, Tuskegee, and Tomotley situated along what is now called the Tennessee River. Though not united, they shared a common cultural heritage and leadership connections.

Over time, Cherokee leaders made an uneasy peace with Blount, but the Chickamauga, a spin-off tribe of the Cherokees originally led by Dragging Canoe and now led by John Watts, continued their raiding parties into Cumberland backcountry. Such Indian attacks escalated retaliation by the American militia, giving the settlers what they understood as just cause for violating existing treaties. Indian towns were burned and villages sacked. An ongoing cautiously guarded relationship between Indians and white settlers continued for decades. Though most Cherokee agreed to peace with Blount, the Creeks, Chickamaugas, and Chickasaws continued defending their homeland against white intrusions; their valuable hunting grounds were disappearing.

Newspaper accounts of scalping and captured white settlers taken by Indians would have fueled Molsey's trepidation of inviting Indians into her home. While Knoxville was growing and being developed, the *Knoxville Gazette* reported numerous Indian attacks and massacres. On June 2, 1792, the newspaper stated, "Within twelve miles of this place, they were picking strawberries, six Indians came up, tomahawked and scalped them, in his view, and went off without making further attempts on the family. What Indians they were is uncertain, but suspicion falls on the Creeks and the Cherokees." A later account on January 9, 1795, revealed:

...myself and family, together with the family of John Titsworth, were attacked by Indians about 12 o'clock at night; my wife, John Titsworth, his wife, one child, and one of my children and one negro were killed on the ground, and captured three of my children, one of John Titsworth's and a negro. Next day, being pursued by Major Maulden and others, they killed and scalped one of my children, and wounded and scalped another of John Titsworth's, then made off with a daughter of mine, about 13 years of age, named Peggy, and a negro boy about 15 or 16 years of age, named Mingo.

These accounts obviously disquieted the residents of Knoxville.

By 1795, the Indians had come to rely on Blount for ammunition. Having given up their ancient weapons, the bow and arrow, they were now entirely dependent on these sons of foreign immigrants, a leverage that reinforced Blount's authority. Blount had invited Cherokee leaders to his mansion in an attempt to solidify peaceful relations. Hoping to put an end to the Indian wars, he had earlier managed to convince the leading chiefs to visit President Washington at Philadelphia in 1794. After that visit, the chief known as Doublehead succeeded in having the annual annuity to the Cherokees raised to $5,000 a year. Within a year of that negotiation, the Cherokees agreed to peace, joining up with the white man. They would often visit the Blounts at their mansion on the Holston River.

J. Ramsey later reported that Molsey's hospitality to the Indians became legendary:

> ...many of the friendly chiefs paid frequent visits to the new capital; and Mrs. Blount became much interested in them, and used her address and persuasion, to induce them to restrain their young warriors from further aggression upon the frontier people. With these she was a deserved favourite.

Even though she had hesitantly agreed to moving to the frontier, she eventually gained a sense of purpose and settled into the role of First Lady. Her refined manner and intelligence complimented William's business and political goals. Ramsey also noted:

> She was an accomplished lady, and she did much to soften and refine the manners of the first inhabitants of Knoxville. Under her administration, a grace and charm was given to the society of the place...the more remarkable and attractive from the external circumstances under which they were, from the necessity of the case, exhibited in the new town upon a distant frontier.

By the time Eliza was born, Molsey had been staying in Knoxville for almost a year. The mansion was probably feeling more like home by then. Her first arrival on the frontier in October of 1792 lasted only six months, after which she returned to North Carolina for almost a year. She went back to Knoxville in the spring of 1794, apparently resolved to make it her permanent home. She had planted gardens—flowers and shrubs—decorated the mansion, and found a place for her favorite musical instrument by the time Eliza was born.

Molsey played a piano forte, a smaller version of the piano. It wasn't practical to have a full-size piano in the Blount Mansion. William had arranged to have a smaller version of a piano brought to the mansion for his wife due to the encumbrance of shipping a full-sized piano over the mountains. Based on the clavichord, the square piano featured a rectangular box that housed the keys and strings. Most of these square pianos were five feet long, one and a half feet wide and eight to ten inches tall. They were supported by simple straight legs and took up a lot less space than a regular full-scale piano. Thomas Jefferson, a friend of William's, had also purchased a square piano for his wife.

Piano forte in the Blount Mansion; possibly played by Molsey Blount.

While William began blueprinting Tennessee's statehood, Molsey planned for more rooms, gardens, and furniture to be added to the mansion. She scheduled social events and planned the education of her children. Richard and Billy attended Reverend Samuel Carrick's school during the day. The boys' education came not only from books in a schoolroom but also from their wild frontier experiences. Later, as the girls grew, they would also be tutored by the Reverend Carrick. This teacher would have taught the boys reading, writing, and how to master all the elements of arithmetic—adding, subtracting, multiplication, and division. The girls, like the boys, would learn how to read and write like their mother had learned, plus become good at playing a musical instrument. Their mother would have made certain to teach them charity, manners, and morals, ensuring they made what Alice Earle in *Home and Child Life in Colonial Days* calls an "imprint of propriety and respectability" in their own families and in society.

William's brother Thomas visited Knoxville, enjoying the company of Molsey's boys. In the company of Blount's favored physician, Dr. Fournier, Thomas and his boys learned all about

Indian life. On August 24, 1795, William wrote his friend saying, "Your son George has lately accompanied my brother Thomas Blount to the Cherokee Nation and has returned well pleased. Dr. Fournoir and my son William were of the party." It was obvious the children were also becoming friendly with the Cherokees.

About this same time, one of Molsey's older girls arrived in Knoxville. Louisa, who had been living with her sister in Tarborough, North Carolina, joined her parents at the mansion. Nancy remained with her uncle Thomas, probably because she had a nearby beau; she later traveled to Knoxville after her father died. The exact time or year that Louisa arrived at Knoxville can only be guessed since it is not recorded in any history. She may have returned with her mother to Tennessee after one of Molsey's many trips back to North Carolina, or perhaps William brought her back with him to Tennessee after one of his many sojourns back east. Most likely Louisa arrived at her parents' home overlooking the Holston River while she was in her teens. The Blount home was certainly overflowing.

In May of 1795, William began selling off some of his younger slaves to make more room. The 1797 census indicated that he owned twenty-seven slaves. It's likely that these slaves lived away from the mansion house, probably in slave quarters situated behind the mansion toward the river, or on farmland used for food production for the family. All through the course of William Blount's history, slaves were crucial in the operation of his holdings. History never mentions that William made money by engaging in the deliberate buying and selling of slaves, plus the Blounts were renowned for treating their slaves well. In May of 1795, William Blount organized a change in the lives of two young slaves.

A friend of William's, Mr. Allison, was involved in discharging a bond or debt he owed to someone else as part of a business transaction. The *William Blount Papers* indicate that Blount arranged the disposition of two young slaves as part of that transaction in a way that would keep the children together. He wrote his friend, stating:

> I'm provided with a likely boy or your Fellow to discharge Allison's bond to you. Also have a sister of his, 16 yrs. of age, likely, healthy & well grown, which you may have as well. Col. King who purchased them from James Guthrie, and has had them in possession sometimes, speaks well of these. They cost $500 dollars. The girl wishes to get with her brother, & for this reason & no other do I wish it may suit you to take her.

It appears that William Blount sincerely cared about the outcome of these young slaves.

He also diligently worked to dispense his duties as Governor, setting his eyes on an eventual transition of the territory into a state. Blount had announcements published in the *Knoxville Gazette* regarding future plans for a constitutional convention for statehood. Molsey, aware of his future goals, would have greeted and entertained various politicians, investing herself actively in the process of "erecting the territorial government into an independent state." Her experience as a politician's wife provided a sense of sophistication to the prospering town of Knoxville. Dillion's *Blount Mansion: Tennessee's Territorial Capital* declares that Molsey ensured that her home functioned as the "social and political center of the Southwest Territory" as it moved toward statehood. The *Tennessee Historical Quarterly* noted the Blounts' providential influence. "Formal receptions and balls, or dances, attended by richly clad ladies and gentlemen, added touches of social glamor to the pioneer community; and, politically, much important business was transacted in the home or office."

While Molsey and William represented the glamour of the pioneer community, a contrasting view of early Knoxville is offered by James Weird, a traveler who visited the area. His description of the town is important, representing a more balanced view of

Knoxville as a frontier town. This different perspective stands engraved on a memorial monument in Volunteer Landing Park, near the Blount Mansion. In 1798, he noted:

> In the infant town of Knoxville the houses are irregular and interspersed. It was county court day when I came. I saw men jesting, singing, swearing, women yelling from doorways. Whiskey & peach brandy were cheap. The town was confused with a promiscuous throng of every denomination —blanket-clad Indians, leather-shirted woodsmen, gamblers hard-eyed & vigilant. I stood aghast. My soul shrank back to hear the horrid oaths & dreadful indignities offered to the Supreme Governor of the Universe...there was what I never did see before on Sunday, dancing, singing & playing of cards. It was said be a gentlemen of the neighborhood that the devil is grown so old that it renders him incapable of traveling & that he has taken up in Knoxville & there hopes to spend the remaining part of his days...as he believes he is among friends.

The original sixteen blocks of what would be Knoxville was surveyed by Charles McClung in 1791 and divided into four lots each, resulting in sixty-four half-acre lots. William purchased several of these lots. Blount Mansion was constructed on lot 18, not a large amount of land for the wealthy land speculator. However, he also owned numerous acres apart from his home, which he utilized for supplying the timber for his mansion, food for his family, and pastureland for crops. As previously mentioned, without a stable of horses on the mansion property, the Blounts would have used the horses of their neighbor, John Chisholm, whenever they needed to travel. Working as an Indian agent for Blount, Chisholm was one of Knoxville's first tavern keepers. The Chisholm Tavern was situated next to the mansion and nearer to the river, a convenient inn for visitors and dignitaries who visited the Blounts.

Molsey would have shopped at the Cowan Brothers Store, the first mercantile store to sell merchandise shipped in by wagons from Richmond, Baltimore, and Philadelphia. Though somewhat isolated on the frontier, Knoxville would eventually attract architects and physicians, along with its share of lawyers and bankers, bookkeepers and tailors. Historian McArthur declares in *Knoxville's History: An Interpretation* that by the mid to late 1790s, the town hosted "ten stores & seven taverns, besides tippling Houses, one Court House, [and] no prison which they boast of as not being an article of necessity." It would not have a church building until after 1800. Religious services were held in the courthouse or local taverns.

Molsey would remain in Knoxville until late 1796, when she returned once more to her homeland, North Carolina. Knoxville was slowly becoming the "cultural, commercial, and social capital of East Tennessee," as McArthur sees it. Yet it was not enough to influence Molsey to stay permanently. She journeyed back over the mountains whenever William returned east. She was lauded as the dark beauty of Blount Mansion, one who brought "refinement and civilization," according to Ramsey, to a town described by McArthur as "nasty, brutish and short." Yet her next journey back to North Carolina was complicated and injurious to her, leaving her children behind and her husband alone.

14

July 1797—Wake County, North Carolina

The scorching July wind insisted on dislodging her neatly arranged hair, tossing dust into the carriage. Molsey squinted into the glare of the seething summer heat, wishing now that she had waited until William could have joined her. He would have insisted that she ride in their new barouche instead of her favored calash. The collapsible hood of the carriage hung above the seat, barely shielding her and her two daughters Eliza and Barbara from the blistering sun. Traveling back to Knoxville meant a seemingly endless jouncing ride over the mountains, but this time was different. The road had been improved, and the threat of Indians had abated. Besides, Col. James King rode ahead, ensuring her safety as he accompanied her back home to Tennessee.

William's last letter had indicated he had to stay in Philadelphia. Molsey couldn't keep from silently beaming ear to ear at the thought of her husband, the new Tennessee State Senator; she felt her heart would burst with pride at his accomplishments, including leading the frontier into statehood a year ago. Oh, how she recalled the chaotic excitement and tension of last year's proclamation of statehood. All the wearying busyness and labor, all the frenetic noise and confusion had been worth the sacrifice. Tennessee was now the sixteenth state. John Adams was the current President of the continental states, and her husband, in the capital, was collaborating with other senators to establish the United States of America. She sighed happily and smiled.

A calash carriage, popular in colonial times and owned by the genteel class such as the Blounts.

Waves of heat washed over her road-weary body as she leaned her head back against the seat. Her children had quieted and appeared to be nodding off to the rhythmical beat of the horses' hooves. She was content. She had just left visiting with her oldest daughter, Nancy, in Tarborough. It wouldn't be long now before she would be united once more with her other children at home in Knoxville. Molsey noted the harmonious echoing hoof beats of the slave carriage behind her; Hagar, Venice, and Cupid were returning with them. Their wagon moved stealthily westward, stuffed with her boxes and trunks. She fairly admitted to herself that she actually missed the mansion and the busy little town of Knoxville. How long had it been since she'd left? She sleepily counted off the months, coming to the conclusion that it had been near ten months. Amazed, her eyes flew open, immediately fixing her focus on the trees speeding too quickly past.

They were going way too fast! Something was terribly wrong. The sound of the horses' hooves on the gravel was pounding. Gone was the steady rhythmical beat she had been lost in. Bolting upright, Molsey called anxiously to her driver, Sam. He grunted, barely coherent, obviously fighting to control the carriage. The precipitous wooded road leading into the hollow relentlessly tugged the carriage into its grip. Molsey's motherly instincts took hold, and she grasped her children tight, screaming at Sam to stop the carriage, to rein in the horses, but nothing she yelled out made a dent. The carriage was completely out of control and wildly careening down the sheer embankment. No matter how desperately hard he pulled on the drag, Sam could not slow the carriage. He leaned wildly forward and backward on his wooden dickey box, nearly losing his footing and falling off while he pulled on the reins, vainly trying to stop the horses and gripping the dragshoe (breaking device).

The dragshoe wasn't working! Sam slammed it against the wheels, driving splinters into his hands, but the mechanism refused to slow the carriage. The horses, pushed down the hill by the incessant force and weight of the carriage, raced to keep ahead of it. Their harnesses clapping and heaving, they galloped frantically, foam dripping from their straining, sweating muscles, outrunning the carriage's unrelenting pursuit. Panic rose biliously in her throat as Molsey braced her feet against the dashboard, tightly clutching her terrified girls. They were screaming, adding to her sense of helplessness.

Sam bellowed above the cacophonous clamor, "Hold on, dere's curb up dere!" Molsey bounced violently to the carriage floor, taking the girls with her. Struggling to regain her seat, she clung to the side of the door. The carriage wheels scraped along a stone wall, and Molsey braced best she could for the crash. Flinging her body over her girls, she lost her footing and balance, and the world went black.

Sam flew off the dickey box (driver's seat), thrown into the grass. Barbara and Eliza were crying and bleeding, nasty cuts all over their faces and hands, dresses torn as their bodies sprawled in the weeds. They lay among the thistles and ragweed, whimpering and dazed. Everything lay scattered about in broken and shattered pieces, thrown from the carriage when it exploded against the tree.

Sam staggered to his feet, bent crooked in pain and holding his arm. The slave wagon slammed to a stop amidst a cloud of dust and dirt in the middle of the hazardously steep road, its members jumping off and running to help wherever they could. Hagar called urgently for her mistress while others searched for the children. She gathered her skirts around her lumbering legs, rushing toward the cries and wails. She found Barbara sitting up in the weeds, blood dripping from her matted forehead and little Eliza sobbing alongside her. Eliza was obviously scared and dirty but seemingly unhurt. Hagar plopped herself down on the ground next to the girls, stroking their backs and cooing words of strength and comfort to them. After a bit, she looked up, querying the others, "Where's da mistress?"

Colonel King, hearing the screaming and the sound of heavy horse beats, had turned back. As he came around the bend in the road, his eyes widened at the sight of the chaos and wreckage spread across the road and into the trees. Cupid, leaning on an upturned carriage wheel, turned around, waving his hat at King. Where was Molsey? From where Cupid stood, Molsey was not to be seen. He gestured to Hagar, shaking his head in indication he didn't know where Molsey was; she wasn't in the carriage.

Urgently waving at the slaves, King shouted to Cupid and the others, "Go find her! Now!" The slaves moved haltingly, uncertain where to start. The wooded hill was extremely steep, providing little safety for their search. Fragments of the carriage and parts of a wheel lay scattered along the road and down the hill. One by one, they looked worriedly at each other, unsure of what had happened and what to do. King angrily kicked his horse. He'd show them what to do. He reached for his whip.

Hagar wished someone—anyone—would help her, help the children, help her mistress. The forest ignored her thoughts, detached, standing by in its breezy silence, unwilling to care, to participate. A shroud of helplessness oozed between the trees, reaching its fingers toward the slave, consuming any sense of direction or action. Hagar attempted to stand, to carry the children to the wagon. Fear and hopelessness moved with her, holding her up. Both Eliza and Barbara were frightened and hurt, in need of solace.

The search for Molsey began. The woods were ghastly silent— no groans, no pleadings, no voices calling for help. Stumbling over roots and rocks, Cupid made his way downhill, holding on to saplings and broken limbs. The darkness of the canopied forest chained his fear. Sliding on wet leaves, he stumbled over a rock, falling on his back. Turning his head, he caught sight of what appeared to not belong. Brushing the clinging damp leaves from his clothes, he sat upright. It was something out of place. It was the mistress, so very still, seemingly dead. Abruptly overwhelmed with fear and panic, he hollered up the hill.

The other slaves, falling and tumbling down the hill, arrived and slowly, fearfully approached her body. Pushing each other ahead, no one wanted to be the first to reach the mistress. From several feet away, she lay with her head on a rock, one arm pinned between two rocks, the other arm at odd angles to her body; her feet and legs were twisted, covered in leaves and debris. Was she breathing? King arrived, out of breath, shouting at the trees, the rocks, the leaves, the slaves—anyone and anything. He literally fell from his horse, running as fast as he could, tripping over every unwanted obstacle, to the limp form of his charge. Kneeling, he felt for a pulse. She was alive, but barely.

The devastating and almost fatal carriage accident in July 1797 left Molsey Blount with months and months of recovery and incredible pain and discomfort. It would also prevent her from returning to her home in Knoxville for quite a while. By the time she finally returned to the Blount Mansion, she had been away from several of her children and her home for one and a half years.

The accident occurred close to Raleigh, North Carolina, on or about July 11, 1797. Molsey had left the area "to avoid if possible the fevers so frequent at this place," as stated in volume 3 of the

John Gray Blount Papers. The details of her accident are missing in the history books. It is only through the words of her husband and her brothers-in-law that the difficulty she and her family suffered is revealed. John Gray Blount reported to a friend in November of 1797, found in the *Blount Papers* that "at Raleigh on her way to Knoxville the Horses run away with the Carriage broke that to pieces & broke her arm, the last news she was doing well." Unfortunately, she was not doing well.

Her carriage had overturned, violently throwing her and her little girls to the ground. Her wounds were extensive. There is no record of what happened to the children. The major complication for Molsey involved a broken arm. The Blount Papers tell us the details of the tragedy that occurred on her return trip home. William mentioned to a friend that "her arm was dreadfully shattered by a Fall from a Carriage" and later he stated that "to find her wound is still so bad as will not permit her to come to me this Winter." The severity of her wound and lengthy recovery suggests that Molsey suffered a compound fracture of her arm. Historical probability holds that her treatment would consist of some type of splinting, cleansing of the wound, and immobility of the arm. She would have also suffered bruising and bleeding.

There are two types of fractures, the most severe being a compound fracture, where the bone is not only broken but protrudes through the skin. The complication of an open wound in colonial times was worsened by a lack of medical knowledge regarding infections. Today, as Jonathan Cluett presents in *Open Fractures*, "surgery is immediately performed to clean the area of the injury…debris and infection can travel to the fracture location, and lead to a high rate of infection in the bone. Once an infection is established, it can be a difficult problem to solve." We know that after a year's recovery, Molsey was still barely able to travel home.

Her husband impatiently waited for her recovery, having briefly visited her in August and September on his journey back to Knoxville. She spent almost all her recovery at the home of Col. Ben Williams of Raleigh. Williams was a longtime political ally of

Blount and graciously offered his Raleigh home for Molsey, who was injured while in Raleigh.

Throughout their time apart, William was heard to say in volume 3 of Masterson's work, "I am extremely oppressed with the Misfortune of my dear Molsey..." and "...a Fall from a Carriage which as yet has delayed her arrival at this place but I now daily expect her with my little daughters..." He anxiously waited for word from his wife or from his brothers throughout the winter of 1797–1798.

Finally, in the latter days of June 1798, she was able to return home. William was unable to accompany his wife on her return trip to Knoxville in July, so Col. James King, a family friend and land agent for William, went to Raleigh to escort her back to Tennessee. King, one of the first settlers in Knoxville, was also a friend of Sevier and owned an ironworks in Tennessee.

Returning to the years prior to her carriage accident, Molsey had left Knoxville in late 1796, during a time of tremendous change for the town. Her husband had ushered in statehood for his Territory South of the River Ohio. She had watched as John Sevier became the new Governor and William the first Senator to represent the new state of Tennessee in the nation's capital. Blount College had been established in Knoxville and Blount County, each named for William. Grainger County, Maryville, TN., along with Fort Grainger at the mouth of the Tennessee River, were named in honor of Molsey.

After leaving Knoxville in 1796, the Blounts' carriage headed for North Carolina. They stopped in Tarborough to pick up his brother Thomas and his wife and to visit with family. The foursome then traveled together to Philadelphia, intent on viewing the inauguration of John Adams in March of 1797. Both brothers represented their states: William was now the Senator from Tennessee; Thomas represented North Carolina. William again basked in the prestige that came with another political office. Molsey enjoyed the opportunity to visit her family and a reprieve from the frontier.

Exactly which children stayed in Knoxville or accompanied their parents back to North Carolina is unclear. Certainly Nancy was still in Tarborough with her aunt and uncle. Louisa was most likely in Knoxville by then. Billy, Richard, and Jacob apparently stayed behind in Knoxville since the historical record later reveals that William enrolled the boys in school during Molsey's absence. That leaves Barbara, four, and, Eliza one, both too young to be without their mother. Because of their young ages, Molsey took her youngest daughters with her.

Molsey and William thoroughly enjoyed their visit to Philadelphia. Masterson relates that "the Blounts were an attractive couple who moved with grace and pleasure in the round of plays, balls, dinners, and receptions." Some concern was noted in Masterson's words regarding Molsey's health: "Despite the tragedy and danger of a miscarriage Mrs. Blount entered into all possible social life of the capital, where her graces drew grudging admiration even from stanch Federalist Justice Iredell." Was she pregnant again? She had delivered her last baby in 1795, approximately two years previously. By the spring of 1797, she was only thirty-six, still of child-bearing age. Whether she was pregnant or not is unknown. It is a fact that her last child born alive was Eliza. After her carriage accident, she did not have another child.

During her travels to North Carolina, Molsey had been able to visit with her mother, arranging for her to move to Tennessee in the spring. She also spent time with her daughter Nancy in Tarborough. At sixteen years of age, Nancy had grown into a young woman, continuing to prefer her home with her aunt and uncle. Molsey's youngest daughters would have enjoyed spending time with their oldest sister. Nearly twenty years apart in age, Barbara had been a baby when Nancy last saw her, and Eliza was barely a year old during this visit.

Another fascinating detail involves the timing of her carriage accident and the beginning of her husband's problems in Congress. As Blount took up his new position as a Tennessee senator to the Philadelphia Senate, his secretive and dubious dealings back home began to catch up with him. On July 7, 1797, Congress completed their investigation of Blount's questionable and illegal activities outside Congress. The United States government began impeachment proceedings against Blount for his dealings with the British. Of interest is the fact that William was expelled from the Senate, literally running from Philadelphia, at the same time that his wife had an accident. Is there any connection? Was she upset and driving the carriage recklessly by herself? Was she leaving North Carolina, embarrassed by her husband's actions, distraught, driving too fast? Had someone sabotaged her carriage? It remains for future historians to try and disassemble any truth behind this coincidence.

What is known is that Molsey's life changed from one of well-being and vigor to one of disability and devastation. From July of 1797 until June of 1798, she was immobilized and struggling to recover from a near-fatal accident. Living at the Raleigh home of one of William's cohorts, Ben Williams, she was well-cared for and eventually recovered. In all probability, she stayed at the Williams' home due to its proximity to her accident. History does not reveal where her little girls stayed. Most likely, a Blount relative brought them to their home in the Tarborough or Washington area.

While the Blounts were in North Carolina, a foreign dignitary visited Knoxville, possibly expecting to meet the Blounts. The future King of France, Louis Philippe, had come to Knoxville on April 29, 1797. Though some historians report that the future king visited the mansion and met the Blounts, he did not. William was in Philadelphia; Molsey on her way home before her accident.

Louis Philippe's opinion of Knoxville would not have pleased the Blounts. He stated in his *Diary of My Travels in America:*

> Still nasty, inhospitable country, sparsely settled. We reached Knoxville early. It would be quite picturesque if not for the wearying regularity of streets and houses in

American towns. The Holstein river, which flows below the town, is broad and beautiful. We bathed in it; the day was very hot. Five years ago there was not a single house here. Now there are over one hundred.

Louis Philippe remained in the Knoxville area for barely a day, possibly unimpressed with its hospitality. He continued:

We are lodging in one of the oldest, but laziness has so pervaded the way of life that they have not yet plugged up the holes in the outer walls cut for scaffolding when they built the house. There are five of these openings in our room, and scarcely a whole pane in the windows. Our horses are indifferently cared for, but the common board is not bad.

He moved on to Maryville, Tennessee, the town south of Knoxville, named for Molsey Blount.

Meanwhile, as Molsey recovered in North Carolina, William worked his way back to Knoxville, taking the back roads in order to evade the hostile creditors and populace that wanted to arrest him and return him to Philadelphia to stand trial. Fortunately for Blount, Congress accepted his bail, and he was allowed to finish his journey to Tennessee unharmed. In time, Blount approached Knoxville in September of 1797. Surprisingly, his popularity in Tennessee had remained untarnished.

With help from his friends, he was welcomed, cheered, and escorted with honors to his mansion. Though disgraced in the east and nearing financial ruin, he managed to maintain a façade of affluence and influence. It wasn't long before Tennesseans were attempting to have him reinstated as their senator in the next election.

Without Molsey with him, William maintained a hero's image as health and age began to take its toll in his daily living. His eyesight deteriorated, and he suffered from fever and ague, lost thirty pounds, and was racked by rheumatism. His friend Dr.

Fournier moved into the mansion to oversee his care in Molsey's absence.

Committed to staying in Knoxville, his wife's absence wore heavily on William, yet he still managed to hide information regarding his future from her. In a letter dated November 17, 1797, he begged his brother John in Washington, North Carolina, to check on his wife, "...pay her such attention as your own Business & Difficulties will permit you." He added, "I do not wish you to mention to Molsey my suggestions of going to Cumberland..."

John Gray Blount, still living in North Carolina, was often called upon to care for William's family members. During Molsey's recovery, he would frequently visit her, overseeing her financial needs and questionable health. William desired that John move to Knoxville in the coming year. Although he pleaded with him, John remained in Washington, North Carolina, for the rest of his life.

Nancy, Barbara, and Eliza were also living in North Carolina during their mother's convalescence. It's very possible that after the accident, the youngest Blount girls went to live with their oldest sister, Nancy, in Tarborough. As 1798 approached, William made plans for the return of his immediate family and for his mother-in-law to move into the mansion.

Mrs. Grainger, Molsey's mother, had remained in North Carolina when her daughter moved over the mountains and now planned on moving back into the Blount household in early 1798. William told his brother, "...I wish Mrs. Grainger to be prepared to come out in the Spring with her Negroes." She was approaching her sixty-ninth year, an age when elderly parents needed support from family and wanted to be close to their grandchildren.

Finally, in June of 1798, Molsey was ready to return home. This would be her last voyage between North Carolina and Knoxville. Because of miscommunication and possible health delays, she finally left Raleigh, stopping in Chapel Hill to visit her nephews. William sent his doctor, Fournier, to escort Molsey and her slaves back home; they arrived in late June. She and the children, under the scrutiny and delight of Knoxville residents, rode into Knoxville, relieved to finally be reunited with the other children and with William. Willie, William, Billy, Richard, Jacob, and probably Louisa embraced Molsey, Barbara, and Eliza after being separated for over a year. Molsey was thirty-seven years old and weak, though recovered and happy to be home. She would never again leave Knoxville, never bear any more children, and never be a long-standing politician's wife. Every aspect of her life had been irrevocably altered. The windows of opportunity were beginning to close.

15

March 8, 1800—Knoxville, Tennessee

Something was very wrong; her mother was still abed. She always rose early, fetching her tea, settling herself out in the sunshine. No one had seen her today. With a rising sense of dread interspersed with caution threatening to overwhelm her, Molsey went to find her. Slowly, she stepped around the doorway to the hall. The fireplace flames flickered red and orange in the early morning chill. She saw a form in the bed—the bundled shape of her mother.

As she approached the feather bed, a definitive moan met her ears. Mary Grainger turned slowly to face her daughter, groaning. Molsey noted the beads of sweat on her forehead. She bent to her mother, pressing her hand to her brow. Not only was she fiery hot to the touch, she was shaking with chills. Fear rising within to grasp her heart, Molsey pressed a hand to her mouth, stifling a gasp. Where was the doctor? She feared the worst. She must find him— now. Thoughts crashed into each other as she bolted from the room, knocking over the candle-stand.

Frantic to find help, to find someone, anyone, she ran shouting, calling to William. From a distance, she heard her husband's muffled reply. He was in his office. He leaned out the doorway, watching as Molsey ran down the steps like water running over a broken dam. Out of breath and in hysterics, she told her husband they needed the doctor immediately; her mother was extremely sick. Signaling Jack, William ordered him to find the doctor and bring him to their house at once.

William did his best to calm his wife, but Molsey had thoughts only for her mother. Pacing the floor of William's office, she fretted about her mother's comfort, her health, her life. Her mother had only lived with her a little over a year ago when she moved from North Carolina to Knoxville. Frail and aging, Mrs. Grainger needed the support and care of her daughter and her family. But now, oh god! She showed signs of that dreaded fever, the one that was killing so many people in Knoxville. The pestilence that swept over her friends and family like a dark, billowing thundercloud was creeping into her home.

The doctor finally came and was instantly ushered to Mrs. Grainger's bedside. He somberly shook his head, offering no hope for recovery. He spoke quietly about how Mrs. Grainger's headache and nausea presaged the progression of the fever. Malaria was an all-too-familiar nemesis in the Blount household. William had suffered reoccurring bouts of this fever for years, as had their children.

In fact, Billy and Louisa had recently complained of not feeling well too. The doctor left instructions for Molsey to make her mother as comfortable as possible as he patted her hand in dismissal. He was usually so helpful, but now his demeanor spoke of disheartenment and resignation. He silently left the parlor as Molsey felt the solitude of grief seep into her soul. What would she do if her dear mother died? Clouds of morbid fear blew into the house.

March had been perpetually overcast with clouds, bringing dread and despair to the mansion. Her mother remained unable to leave her bed, fatigued and overcome with fever, vomiting, chills, and more fever. Her children, her mother—all were ailing. A sense of helplessness and foreboding spread through the house, choking her family and leaving her wasted. Worn out and exhausted, Molsey wearily wandered from bed to bed, mopping brows and offering water. She insisted on pushing through her weariness, always ready to hold a hand or say "I love you."

The next day she couldn't escape the knowledge that her mother was slipping away, weakened and feverish with malaria, unable to eat or drink. Molsey slowly walked to the hall. She stopped in midstep. It was too quiet, tomblike, with a chill stillness that hadn't been there before. Slowing, forcing her feet forward, she neared her mother's bed. Looking carefully at her mother, scanning her aged body for movement, she froze, no longer able to fight back the rush of grief that anxiety had been forcing upon her. Her mother wasn't breathing. Numbness joined hands with denial as she ever so gently and carefully touched her mother's cheek. Denial and stark fear drove her from the bed. Her mother was dead. Her world whirled out of control as she haltingly backed out of the room. Hugging herself, she stumbled to her bedroom, collapsing on her own bed.

Hagar heard the sobbing and found Molsey sprawled on the bed, lost in her tears and the agony of grief. She knew this grief. Walking to her mistress, she settled beside the bed, patting back and shoulders as they shuddered in racking, heaving wretchedness. Ever so slowly the sobbing eased, spent, and Molsey turned, asking for William. Hagar rose and left to find her master. He would know what to do. Molsey didn't want to be anywhere but on her bed.

Molsey remained in bed that day. William made the preparations for his mother-in-law's burial the following day. Having died on Sunday, March 9, he had to work quickly to find wood for a coffin; Sam would know how to make one. As he made notes to himself, he wiped his brow with a weary hand, feeling chilled and weak. He had to stay strong to complete the last honor given to Molsey's mother, even though he was feeling ill and wondered if he too was falling into the clutches of another bout with malaria.

On March 9, 1800, Mary Grainger died in Knoxville from malaria. She was seventy-one years old and had only lived at the mansion for a little more than a year. She either arrived shortly after Molsey returned from her long convalescence or came with Molsey from North Carolina at the same time. She was a welcomed member of the family, having lived before with the Blounts in North Carolina. Yet in late 1799 and 1800, a deadly, fatalistic disease in the late eighteenth century, malaria, was epidemic in Knoxville, killing many residents.

It's not known where Mrs. Grainger is buried. However, as the mother of a prominent politician's wife, her burial would have been held with pomp and ceremony. Numerous neighbors and friends of the Blounts would have attended. William did not record her death in his writings, but a business colleague, John Sevier, noted simply in his journal for March 11, 1800, "Mrs. Granger buried." Confused as to the exact date of death, John Summerville, a confidential Blount agent, reported that she was buried on March 10, 1800. The *John Gray Blount Papers* state in a letter to Thomas Blount, contrary to Sevier's note, "On the 10th, instant Mrs. Grainger was buried after a short illness of bilious fever..." Most likely, she died on March 9, 1800, and was buried the next day.

She was one of many of Knoxville's residents who succumbed to the ravages of this dreaded fever that year. Transmitted by mosquitoes, malaria was ubiquitous on the frontier. With various incubation periods, the colonial citizens did not understand how it was transmitted, let alone how one prevented the illness. No one could predict who would live and who would die. Even so, it was well-known that the frail elderly and young infants and children were more susceptible to these diseases. Malaria symptoms can appear in cycles and may come and go over time.

Molsey's accustomed response to the debilitating grief of loss was to go to bed and stay there for days, and so it is that history finds her in bed, mourning the loss of her mother. A Blount letter states, "...during her sickness, Mrs. Blount was confined a day or two." Two of her children's lives were in jeopardy at the time this was going on: "Miss Louisa had a severe attack for three days, but is now in perfect health." Billy, six, had also become extremely ill, "attacked with a very violent bilious fever, which had nearly cost him his life…" The whole of the Blount mansion was infected with malaria. Molsey was overwhelmed by constant fear and dread, but it had not always been so tumultuous.

Prior to the spring of 1800 and Mary Grainger's death, the winter of 1798–1799 had proven productive for William and exciting for Molsey. Once more, William was making political inroads. Tennesseans had brushed off his impeachment problems. He was busy negotiating the cessation of more Indian lands, and James White's seat in the Tennessee Senate was now open. By October, he had been elected as a Senator to represent Knox County in Nashville. By December he had managed to elevate himself to the position of Speaker of the Tennessee Senate.

Molsey had subsequently gained continued esteem and prestige as the Lady of Blount Mansion. As the former governor's wife, she inherited the respect and admiration of local residents. She frequently entertained political leaders, civic dignitaries, and frontiersmen at the mansion and attended balls and banquets, always on the arm of her admired husband, of course. The *Blount Mansion Interpreter's Manual* describes their elegant home. Overlooking the Holston River, it had become a "beacon of elegance," welcoming both frontiersmen and the rich. The Indians had called it the "house with many eyes" because of its glass windows. Surrounded by a milieu of log homes and forest, the mansion represented change and the "end of the frontier."

John Sevier's diary reflected a myriad of social events and weather reports during this time. For years, the Blounts and Seviers dined and shared teas together. Sevier noted on July 10, 1798, "…very warm Mrs. Sevier & Miss Joanna took tea at Mr. Blounts." Later that month on July 24, Sevier recorded that it had been "…very warm Gov. Blount his Lady, Miss Mary & William took tea." Basking in the company of William and Molsey, Sevier again provided a look at Molsey's life by stating on August 5, 1798, "Myself & Mrs. Sevier accompanied her (Mrs. Sparks) and Mrs. Blount part of the way as far as the sign of Cross Keys."

Molsey finally had all her children in her nest at the Blount mansion by late 1798, except Nancy. As an eighteen-year-old young lady, Nancy had affection for Henry Toole of Tarborough, who would become her first husband around the year of 1809. Though several historical accounts prefer to have Nancy living at the mansion, she met and married Henry in North Carolina, never living in Knoxville. She came to Knoxville when her father died and then only for a visit.

Louisa, sixteen, was living at the mansion in 1798. As a young woman, it wasn't long before she captured the attention of one Pleasant Miller, a Knoxville lawyer and friend of her father's. Molsey's two oldest boys—Billy, then fourteen, and Richard, nine—were under the tutelage of Rev. Samuel Carrick. Young Jacob, seven, would soon attend the same school; Barbara, six, and Eliza, three, remained home, schooled by their mother. Family frequently visited, staying for weeks.

By the fall of 1798, Molsey was invested in her family and Knoxville's social scene. She acquired elegant furniture and household decorations suitable for reflecting the Blount social status and enlarged the home to accommodate the growing family and other relatives.

The original mansion had consisted of two main rooms, a hall and a parlor, and an upstairs attic and small basement. Eventually, the mansion expanded to include a full downstairs bedroom, which was made by moving and attaching the former slave quarters to the main house. William's office was separate from the house, as was the kitchen. Molsey supervised the furnishing of the mansion, which today reflects her genteel taste and "modern" conveniences. Though she did not decorate the rooms ornately, they reflect the sophistication of an important family coupled with the functionality necessary in frontier Knoxville.

Blount Mansion: cellar room fireplace, possibly part of original structure.

Molsey had been a plantation wife in North Carolina. She had been schooled as a young girl in manners, entertaining, and the proper foods to serve guests. She was expert in supervising meal preparations, the candle making, and household chores. The late eighteenth century heralded changes in cultural traditions centered around colonial tables. As the *Blount Mansion Interpreter's Manual* stated, Molsey enjoyed the newer custom of the hostess remaining at the dinner table during the meal. "...unlike her grandmother, she did not serve the food directly to her guests (an activity that literally required the hostess to have eaten prior to the meal so that time could be spent serving guests.)" In that way, she could remain seated with her guests, involved in their company.

The Blount Mansion kitchen was a separate small building, close to the house. Molsey would have overseen the preparation of all the food from this kitchen.

After dining at the mansion, guests would retire to the more formal parlor. According to *The Blount Mansion Manual*, the parlor was small, yet a room to "show-off ones wealth and social status," the parlor was used for various occasions such as "weddings, christenings, funerals, and sitting with the body," but Molsey's ease of life would soon change.

While the Blounts maintained a social position of wealth and privilege, the façade was crumbling. For decades Blount had invested and speculated on millions of acres of land and had acquired a vast fortune of businesses, naval stores, and shipping routes with his brothers. By 1798, he had overextended himself. His millions of acres were losing value, and he was struggling to avoid bankruptcy. Always a clever businessman, Blount came up with a scheme to escape being penniless. In an effort to escape the loss of all he owned, he deeded the mansion and all his assets to his brother Willie.

Willie Blount, Molsey's brother-in-law. He became the guardian to her children upon William's death in March 1800 and eventually the owner of the Blount Mansion.

Though this action protected his assets while he was alive, it left Molsey and her children at the mercy of Willie if anything happened to William. Therefore, by 1799, the Blount Mansion and all its contents had been transferred to Willie's ownership. An inventory list, compiled by Blount, gives historians a clear look at the Blounts' wealth.

With his fortunes transferred to his brother and his wife back home in Knoxville, the Tennessee Senator began to entertain national politics again. Perhaps he could run again for the position of Senator from Tennessee and return to the nation's capital. Molsey was resettled into the routines of her Knoxville home and caring for her children, plus her mother was part of her household, always a comfort to Molsey. The family seemed to be returning to a comfortable lifestyle with a promising future, but Death had other plans.

16

April 1800—Knoxville, Tennessee

Darkness prevailed, blanketing her, but not with warmth. Nothing she did or didn't do dispelled the heavy curtains of depression and grief that threatened to drown her. She pecked at her food, spoke only when spoken to, and bemoaned the deep chasm left by their deaths. Dread of another day, another moment without her beloved mother and husband kept her chained to her bed. For all their pleas and enticements, not even her children could bring her to the table. She wooed death, desiring nothing more than to fall into the canyon of eternity. Her husband's death, close on the coattails of her mother's, had removed all sense of completeness and purpose. Feeling buried in the soil of hopelessness, she lay staring at the dust particles drifting in the sliver of lingering sunshine invading her bedroom.

Nothing else mattered. Her longing to clasp death to her heart matched the ebony emptiness in her soul. Thoughts, caught like a fluttering fly in the web, desperately struggled in the battle between life and death. Sorrow kidnapped her soul and dragged her into a putrid place of doubt and denial.

She screamed inside herself, "God, no no! God! Why? Why did he have to die? Why did you take my mother?" Rolling to face the wall, she clutched the bedclothes about her and sank into oblivion.

No one could console her, though everyone tried. Louisa, a young lady of eighteen, slipped into the bedroom, bringing with her an unwelcome new candle, chasing away the shadows that crept into the cold room. She herself had just recovered from a recent brush with death and longed for her mother's comfort but stoically lay that aside, realizing hers was the role of comforter right now. Billy, now sixteen, stood leaning on the bedroom doorway. A victim of the bilious fever, stricken the day after his grandmother died, he was slowly recovering, still fighting his own battle with that awful illness, needing his mother too. The younger children attempted to approach their mother, only to back away, unsettled by the sight of their mother's anguish and pain.

The mansion barely breathed in the macabre silence. The shuffling feet of the youngest two children vied for recognition as little Eliza and Barbara wandered back from the bedroom. Hagar and Venice worked to occupy them with games of cats-in-the-cradle and blocks. Jacob and Richard sat near their uncle Willie, his casual demeanor playing upon their need for relief and play. The children understood their father's and grandmother's passing better than the adults. They accepted the changes, the grieving, and prepared to move on with life, desiring only that their world return to the sense of normalcy, before their mother had taken to her bed and stayed there.

Neighbors and friends had attended the funerals, only two weeks apart. The Seviers, Whites, Mrs. Chisolm, and Carracks were instantly on hand upon word of William's death with soothing hugs and whispered words of condolence wrapped around warm dishes of steaming food and offers of any help needed. All had been bereaved at one time or another, such was the natural rhythm of life, albeit unexpected at times, but none had faced such devastating deaths so close together. Willie had moved into the mansion to oversee the care and running of the mansion and as guardian of William's children.

Molsey would have to return to her role as mother. Her other aspects, the roles of wife and daughter, were suddenly and inexplicably gone. What would her life be like without William, without her mother? For days and weeks, her heart, mind, and soul wrestled with those answers. Retreating to her bed had been her way of dealing with grief and pain for her whole life. Her bed had always been her refuge, the one place she could wrap herself up and ignore the biting reality of her harsh and unrelenting misery.

Had it been a few weeks since their deaths? She couldn't tell. It seemed the cold despair would never release her. A thought flickered through the bottomless pit of her mind: was she being selfish by refusing to get up, to get dressed, to embrace the needs of her children? She sighed. "Maybe tomorrow. Maybe..." The drowning envelope of sleep welcomed and warmed her.

April had always been that special time of hope, flushed in the creeping blush of spring that somehow managed to always burst forth, suddenly full of budding dogwoods and redbud trees lacing the forests around their home, Blount Mansion. Molsey's garden greedily drank in the sunshine and promised rows of color, beds of herbs, and green leaves for curing aches and pains. New life birthed in the pastures and surrounding woods, not just from the foliage, but with capering foals, shy fawns and bunnies, and bawling baby calves. For Molsey, however, it was different this year; it was a time smudged with endless doubt and longing. Her children's laughter and gay banter haunted the rooms of the mansion, stalking their mother. Their lingering voices soothed her, rallied a lost sense of caring. Slowly, she returned to the breath of youth around her, anticipating the childish giggles and endless queries. It would be the children who became her lifeline, pulling her back to a sense of purpose and infusing meaning to her life.

Willie mentioned that her daughter Nancy was coming to Knoxville, escorted by Ann Blount Harvey, her aunt. She nearly ventured to dare a glimpse at happiness at the thought of Nancy's arrival. Her oldest daughter was finally coming to the mansion! Willie told her that Thomas had agreed to send her to see her mother, hoping her presence would bring comfort to the whole family.

Hagar shuffled from the kitchen toward her mistress with a teapot and plate of scones. She approached Molsey, so hoping she

195

would eat something. The faithful slave had not failed to notice how the bones on Molsey's wrist protruded more and how dark circles had spread beneath her eyes. She knew her job. She had to tend to her mistress, even when Molsey didn't want to be cared for and had lost all taste for nourishment. Molsey nodded her silent thanks at Hagar's intentions, dismissing any further conversation. She noted the scone, covering it up with the napkin. Reaching for the teapot, her mind fluttered in a newfound purpose, how to get Nancy to stay in Knoxville.

Perhaps today she would go to his grave with Willie or someone. She could see what had been done for his burial site. She almost felt stronger just in thinking about the visit, or was it in believing she could be close to him again? She would go to William's grave. She had heard that he was the first buried in a little hillside cemetery plot, part of a field that would eventually become a place for a church someday. But where was her mother buried? She would think about that later.

For now, she wanted to arrange visiting William's grave. Since she hadn't been able to participate in his burial and preparations for his funeral, she now felt the urge to see what others had done for him. Willie's hasty return back from Nashville upon receiving the news of his brother's death still wasn't talked about. Her thoughts collided in her head as she worked out the details of what to wear and who to take with her. Eagerness returned to her soul if just for a while. Once again, she would be with William.

⌒⦿⦿⦿⦿⌒

William Blount died on March 21, 1800, leaving a wife, seven children, and a legacy of question, conflict, honor, and pride. Molsey and William had been married twenty-two years, a time full of separations, losses, elation, and hope. His death terminated his family's well-being and stability. Suddenly Molsey lost all manner of support and guardianship of her children and faced a daunting future. Her husband had escaped impeachment, their fortunes were consumed by bankruptcy, her brother-in-law was in charge of her children, and her mother was recently deceased. She resorted to the only thing she knew to trust after these deaths—her bedroom.

Having just recovered from the dreaded fever, she remained in bed, unable to function. Molsey had little to nothing to do with the burial and funeral of her husband. His burial occurred the day after his death. John Sevier had visited William on March 15, noting the visit in his journal. On March 22, 1800, Sevier wrote, "Went with family to the burial of Mr. Blount." Since he died on March 21, 1800, with Willie still in Nashville, who orchestrated his funeral? Blount was popular and well-known, so it's entirely plausible that several residents of Knoxville made the arrangements. John Summerville would have been an excellent candidate since he was William's confidential agent. He authored a letter to William's brother John Gray, notifying him of his brother's death.

Since Blount died in the early evening hours of March 21, he would have been laid out in the mansion with a family friend or relative sitting up with the body on that evening. Hastily, a funeral was planned for Knoxville's hero. The following day, in the newly formed cemetery at the corner of Arch and Fifth Street (now the corner of State and Church Streets), William was laid to rest. Blount's body was the first to be interred in what would become the First Presbyterian Church's Cemetery, the oldest burial grounds in the frontier town.

With her bed as her sanctuary, Molsey sealed herself off from the rest of the household occupants and any plans for the future. Molsey was probably unaware of the legal and financial complications resulting from her husband's death. Colonial culture demanded that all widows be cared for by other family members. She inherited nothing from William. Adding to the anxiety surrounding William's sudden and unexpected death was the fact that William did not have a will or last testament. Just prior to his death, in an attempt to avoid bankruptcy, he cleverly deeded the mansion, all its possessions, and the immediate Knoxville lands to his brother Willie. William had also been the executor of several estates and partner in a multitude of land holdings within the family and family businesses. Subsequent legal matters would unravel these complex matters and cause angst for the Blount brothers. For Molsey, her mother's death was also problematic. Most confusing was the will left by Mrs. Grainger who had died several days before William.

Molsey's mother had granted her son-in-law, William, the legal right to maintain and oversee her assets, which had included lands and several slaves. Now William was dead, leaving Mrs. Grainger's estate without an executor. William's brothers John and Willie somehow assumed the processing of her estate in Tennessee. Molsey was excluded from this process as her brothers-in-law worked to settle the matter.

In the *John Gray Blount Papers, Volume 3*, two months after both deaths, John Gray Blount sent directions to Willie:

> You will receive herewith the will of Mrs. Granger to which you are an Executor & the only one which can at present act, the property all being where you are and the witnesses all dead or supposed to be so except Reading Blount. If he is dead or out of the State I suppose you must qualify with the will annexed unless the proving by (unreadable)...hand writing will do. But, I suppose that will do as the near finding it amongst her valuable papers would pass (i.e. prove it to be) personal property.

What became of Mrs. Grainger's property is uncertain. Perhaps the answer lies within the historical archives of Willie Blount's papers.

The future of William's children was another area of great concern after his death. Hugh White and Willie were assigned guardianship of Molsey's children. Molsey's life was now at the mercy of her brothers-in-law. In May of 1800, Willie wrote to his brother Jacob:

> I have put my Nephews William, Richard and Jacob to School about ten miles from here under a good teacher...they learn with much ease to themselves anything they attempt the Study of...Barbara goes to school in this town and is sometimes accompanied by Eliza, the principle benefit children of their ages receive at school is to be kept out of mischief and free from contracting bad habits.

There is no mention of the whereabouts of Louisa. Presumably she was still in Knoxville, perhaps living with a family friend.

With three of her children placed in schools ten miles from home, and her younger children—Barbara, eight, and Eliza, six— at a local school, the mansion became a living tomb. For Molsey, it was a most cruel and lonely time. The happy, noisy home of just a few months ago was silenced. Left alone with the slaves and possibly Willie, her future was questionable. By late May or early June that silence was broken; another change was coming to the mansion.

Molsey's oldest daughter, Nancy arrived from North Carolina, accompanied by her aunt Ann Harvey, William's sister. Nancy was questionably ill prior to the journey, probably due to the stress of her father's death. Ann feared for her well-being during the journey to Knoxville. There was another problem for Ann and Nancy prior to leaving for Tennessee, which seems trivial, but important enough for Thomas to mention in a letter to John Gray, dated April 25, 1800. Thomas wrote, "...she appears to be in great distress arising from the difficulty of procuring suitable black Dresses for herself & Nancy Blount. She sent a memo by Reading to you & wishes to know whether it can be complied with...for not an article that she wants can be had here..."

This is the first time that Nancy had traveled over the mountains. The majority of her life was spent with relatives rather than her parents, something which remains a mystery to this day. Still, her devotion to her parents somehow remained intact. Upon her father's death, Nancy was interested in procuring a mourning ring.

A mourning ring was exactly that—a ring, usually forged in gold, memorializing a deceased loved one. These rings could represent an entire family, involving the hair of relatives worked into the design of a specific pattern or the creation of symbols representing special meaning to the wearer. Most rings were made of gold and a combination of onyx or porcelain. There was no standard design or pattern, only the desire to honor the memory of someone who had died. The bearer of the ring would often have the name of the deceased inscribed on the band.

Frequently the living would create rings to leave to their heirs, listing the intended recipients in their wills. In this case, it seems that Nancy had a ring made to honor both her parents. Her aunt stated in a letter she penned to Mrs. John Gray Blount, prior to their visit to Knoxville, "Nancy Blount has sent her ring to Mr. Grove Wright for to get hair put in it of her Fathers & Mothers thare was only M B in it before...she wishes to tell him...to have W M B put in her Ring..." The engraving of "WMB" referred to her father, though he did not have a middle name; later generations were left questioning its meaning.

Molsey remained in the mansion, now owned by Willie, with her children boarded in schools, leaving her days void of family warmth. Her future was tenuous. Apparently, the brothers had discussed her future more than once. In a very long letter to Willie on May 11, 1800, John Gray specifically reinforced what was to become of her children and her financial security. He was interested in assuring that William's land speculations were all sorted out and that Willie followed his directions. John instructs Willie to provide for:

> ...William Blounts Family & the Schooling the Children. I expect the School of adversity has taught to Molsy that

cunning now so necessary & that little will be necessary to maintain them (more than) can be made by the negroes. And from some sources as much must be raised as will School them all particularly the Boys. As I am so much pushed here nothing can be expected from me and if it cannot be done without sacrificies must be made to accomplish that of all others to our Brother in his life time the most desirable. Molsy must give up to you the Boys & they must go the best Schools & have an education.

John had subtly suggested that Molsey needed the difficult lesson of death to learn to be more frugal, or at least to become more appreciative of his brother's efforts. His words seem to have revealed a sense of hostility toward Molsey's previous elite financial position. He alluded to the belief that it was of utmost importance to see that the male children received a good education.

Toward the end of this letter, John assuaged his harsh judgment of Molsey, stating, "You will also please offer to Molsy the most sincere condolence of Polly & myself; I would have written her but my mind is too much embarrassed with a variety of subjects to sooth hers by any observations I can make." Still living in North Carolina, John used the convenience of distance and the possible lack of sincerity for Molsey's grief to avoid addressing her directly. His request of his brother to pass on his condolences spoke more to an obligatory relationship on his part than a sincere compassionate response to his brother's widow.

Molsey was alone in her deep-seated need to regain a normal life. Any adult or family member that meant anything to her was gone. Her parents, husband, and brothers had all died, leaving her to rely solely on her brothers-in-law for financial support. Willie, thirty-two and seven years her junior, took over the operation of the mansion and shared the guardianship of her children with Hugh James White, the son of James White. Her future was bleak.

William's death seemed to have silenced Molsey's voice in the historical record. Except for mention in the letters between the remaining Blount brothers immediately after William's death, she is basically forgotten in history until her death in October of 1802. Her sister-in-law Ann Harvey and her daughter arrived a few months after William had died, yet we don't know how long they stayed. Molsey remained in Knoxville at the mansion, living a solitary life, dressed in the mourning colors of a widow and awaiting her own death.

From left to right, the graves of William Blount, Molsey Blount, Ann Blount Harvey and the young son of Eliza Blount Wiatt. This is the third grave site for William and Molsey.

17

October 7, 1802—Knoxville, Tennessee

The candle flickered, signaling something. Perhaps it was William, he'd returned for her! She stared out from under the bedcovers, scrutinizing the shadows dancing over the wooden walls. Delirious from fever, Molsey longed for her husband. She called out, eager for an answer, fully expecting a voice to call her name, but nothing resounded in the quiet of her bedroom other than her own voice. "He's busy and can't hear me. He's...his office," Molsey whispered, her voice weakened from her illness. She pushed back the woolen covers, grabbing her sides against the cold. She would go to him. He could help her. She was certain he was here. Was she dreaming, or was he really here?

Inching up and to the edge of the feather bed, Molsey tried to stand. She awkwardly labored to gather her strength for another try and, leaning forward, fell on the floor. The dull thud of her sweaty emaciated body hitting the floor summoned her daughter from the hall. Louisa had come to stay with her mother, leaving her own home to care for her that day. She hurried to her distress, struggling to breathe, and tried to lift her from the floor, calling for Hagar.

The ever-faithful aged Hagar managed to awaken from her sleep and grope for a chair to help her get up from the ancient pallet while she steadied herself on her feet. She had been sleeping next to Molsey's bed since her mistress had become sick, though her poor hearing and eyesight seemed to complicate matters. Sincere in her efforts to aid Louisa, Hagar only added to the urgency in the room.

Seeing Molsey's limp, sweaty form lying on the floor struck fear to the core of Louisa's heart. She knew her mother was ill, but she had never seen her so afflicted and certainly never unable to stand. Her mother seemed lost in an illusionary world, chattering about her father and hearing his voice. Louisa grabbed her under the arms, struggling to get Molsey's legs out of the way and keep her nightgown down. Hagar finally made it around the bed, bending down to lift her legs into the bed. The two women eyed each other, unwilling to share their disbelief and panic.

Molsey had been ill off and on but never so incapacitated, so weak and helpless. Doctor Dickson had checked on her just recently, noting with concern the yellow tinge to her skin, along with her lack of appetite and constipation, all of which signaled more than he could cure. During his visits, the doctor had also noted her weight loss. He had previously left instructions for Molsey to eat more, but she had refused most food, sipping occasionally on a cup of tea. She hadn't eaten for days.

Molsey lay back on the cotton pillow, sighing, each breath a singular battle of its own. Icy panic rose in Louisa's throat; she was watching her mother die before her very eyes. Louisa's thoughts overwhelmed her mind as terror seeped into her soul, and she swallowed back the tears that threatened her disbelief. Molsey's eyes were closed, her jaundiced face placid and expressionless. Her breaths came shallower and shallower, shorter and shorter, intermittently sending echoes of the impending death. Forcing a reaction, making her mouth move and words appear, Louisa slowly demanded Hagar, "Go… now…! Doctor…! Go!"

By now the older children had awakened to the shouts and scuffling. Billy and Richard stood in the shadows of their mother's bedroom, holding candles, wondering what had happened. Eight-year-old Jacob climbed down the ladder from the upstairs bedroom, sleepily stumbling toward his brothers. Louisa suddenly had support, had someone to help her. She was no longer alone in this unfamiliar fear and panic. Billy, now eighteen and only two years younger than Louisa, knew nothing of sickness and death.

Still he understood something horrible was happening to his mother.

He came 'round to the far side of the rumpled bedcovers, grabbing for his mother's hand. Molsey didn't even open her eyes. Her demeanor appeared relaxed, resigned, almost content in her veiled consciousness. Billy looked over at Louisa, shaking his head as a tear formed in the corner of his eye. He refused let his sister see him cry.

Outside the bedroom, Richard grabbed his younger brother, Jacob, by the shoulders to prevent him going into their mother's bedroom. Jacob wriggled free, slapping Richard's hand and ducking behind Louisa. Now only Richard was left to enter the room. Richard, like most young people his age, defied life by denying death, but the silence and the pall hanging over the bedroom ensured that he would change his mind. He slowly approached his siblings, taking up a stance at the end of the bed in their guarding of his mother from eternity.

Louisa knelt beside her mother's bed, held her tiny hand, and silently infused her love for her through that touch. Her mother had been so lonely, so depressed for so long after her father had died. Maybe now her mother could be released from a life of longing and despair. Louisa kissed her mother's hand and laid her cheek on it. Jacob, Richard, and Billy stood stoic and silent in their recognition that their mother was dying. No one voiced those words, but an unrelenting tug of an oncoming tide of grief engulfed the room. Molsey's older children gathered in the silent presence of death, waiting for someone to tell them this wasn't happening.

Slam! Their reverie disturbed by the front door, they turned. With a cold night breeze escorting the doctor, he rushed into the bedroom, bringing with him what the children hoped for—life and help for their mother. He asked for more light as he opened his small doctor's bag, leaving it on the floor while he touched her head and checked her pulse. Stepping back, he solemnly shook his head, squeezing Louisa's shoulder. "I'm sorry. There is nothing I

205

can do," he muttered, erasing any hope the children had mustered. "She is close to dying...the jaundice...I'm so sorry," he repeated.

Resuming their watch, Billy, Louisa, Richard, and Jacob kept to their positions around their mother. Molsey's breath was barely detectable. Louisa noted that the two youngest children were still in bed, a place that she wished she was at right now. Barbara and Eliza were too young anyway to be in the room of their dying mother. Louisa glanced at her brothers and wondered to herself what they would all do without their mother. Her mother had always been their strength, their defender, and their inspiration.

Then suddenly, it was over. Molsey gasped once and retreated into eternity. The pall of death was gentle, leaving her with a peaceful expression and regard. Louisa was first to let out a burst of tears, throwing herself over her mother. The boys joined in with their own tears, grasping each other's hands or shoulders. Stumbling toward their mother's body, they clutched each other, reaching for something that no longer existed.

Wails and cries echoed through the mansion. Each child was now an orphan, each struggling to understand their loss and grief. Each consoled the other. Louisa's mind turned in concern about how to tell her younger sisters, Barbara and Eliza. How do you tell a ten-year-old and a seven-year-old that their mother had died in the night? Maybe Uncle Willie would help her. Who else would be there to help them?

The next day dawned like any other day for the residents of Knoxville but not for the Blount children. Their future was now in the hands of relatives. Only two years ago, their grandmother and father had died. Now their mother was gone too, surely a death with huge consequences. But for now, they had to make plans for their mother's funeral.

❦

Molsey Blount died on October 7, 1802, at the early age of forty-one in the Blount Mansion, a home she had lived in for a little over six years of her life. William had died two years previously, and now her children were suddenly orphaned. All her children were living in Knoxville, except for Nancy. The mansion was the center of social events and political importance. After Molsey's death, the family home became a place of uncertainty and despair.

The household slaves and Willie would have stepped up to provide comfort to the children. History reveals that Willie had initially lived in the mansion, but it is unclear if he was living there after his brother William died. Since its construction in 1792–1793, the mansion had undergone massive improvements, its structure enlarged to accommodate children and other family members. Experts differ regarding the years that these changes were made. Some indicate that the small west-wing room attached to the original structure was used as the Blount master bedroom; if it was their bedroom, it would therefore be the room where both Blounts died. It's also possible that this room was the old slave quarters or the original kitchen.

Molsey's last will and testament was never found. When she died, she possessed a few personal items, but the contents of the mansion, slaves, and lands had been willed to Willie in 1797. Thus, it was that Willie took over the operation of the mansion, leaving Molsey living there as his guest. Little mention of her death is noted in the *Knoxville Gazette*. Several months after her death, Willie offhandedly commented to his brother John Gray in a November 19, 1802, letter, "I have by a letter of recent date forwarded by Doctor Dickson informed you of a melancholy event which has happened here, the death of my sister (Molsey) of a complaint called the Jaundice…" With that comment, no further mention of Molsey is made by the Blount brothers.

The cause of her death was noted in historical records as jaundice. Using today's medical diagnosis, jaundice is an indication of liver problems. An early sign of possible liver problems would be a yellowish tint to the skin, indicating an obstruction of bile ducts, fluids, and tissues. Liver problems can occur due to excessive alcohol use, cancer, or hepatitis. Since an affected liver cannot flush toxins from of the body, bilirubin (a yellowish-brown waste product found in bile) builds up, causing the yellow discoloration. Molsey also would have been weak and tired from loss of appetite, abdominal changes, and constipation. Dr. Dickson was her doctor, not Dr. Fournier, William's doctor. According to John Sevier, Dr. Fournier had died in 1799.

Dr. Dickson probably bled Molsey, as was the custom in colonial times. He could have used other treatments, some quite questionable. According to a small booklet published in Williamsburg in 1742, the favored treatment for jaundice was, "Take a live Tench (a freshwater fish), slit it down the Belly; take out the Guts and clap the Tench to the Stomach as fast as possible, and it will cure immediately." Another treatment might have involved a poultice of herbs and healing plants.

Molsey's body would have been washed and dressed by family members or friends. Her burial was arranged for the day after her death. Since William had been buried at the small cemetery that would become the First Presbyterian Church Cemetery, Molsey was laid to rest beside him. She was the third person to be buried in the cemetery, William the first. Grave markers were simple at that time. Over her grave was laid a solid, plain concrete slab engraved with "Mary Blount, Died October 7, 1802, Aged 41 years." Her grave marker is free of any other symbols or flare, similar to William's gravestone. Since neither William nor Molsey had been religiously oriented, their gravestones do not have any crosses, weeping willow trees, or ornate skulls on them. Interestingly, since their burials, their bodies have been moved two more times due to construction of the current church building.

Her death was announced by someone going around and knocking on the doors of those people who knew her, a popular custom at the turn of the century. Information concerning her funeral would be offered at the same time, along with items such as handkerchiefs in accompaniment to the invitations. Her children, John Sevier and his family, and many Knoxville residents attended Molsey's funeral. A funeral hearse draped in black and pulled by horses preceded the way to the cemetery; family and scores of residents followed the coffin borne on the decorated wagon. Since funerals doubled as social events, a gathering would have occurred before or after the funeral, involving a feast of food and discussions concerning the life of the First Lady.

With both William and Molsey gone, the Blount Mansion became eerily quiet. Gone were the dinners, balls, and teas. Only the wanderings of their children and the footsteps of faithful slaves were left. William's legacy was the statehood of Tennessee and the overseeing of the foundation of Knoxville. Molsey's legacy was her children. Almost every single one of her adult children went on to influence the future of Tennessee, or at least the cities of Knoxville and Nashville.

The oldest surviving child at the time of Molsey's death was Nancy Blount. She remained in North Carolina, marrying her first husband, Henry Toole of Tarborough. After his death, she remarried a native of North Carolina, William Hadley. Unfortunately, Nancy died an early death on June 3, 1805, leaving behind three children of her own. She was twenty-five years old.

Louisa Blount wed a Knoxville lawyer, Pleasant Miller, on April 11, 1801, a year after her father's death and a year before her mother's passing. Miller became a prominent Knoxville commissioner. In 1824, he moved his family to Madison County. She died at the age of sixty-five on February 14, 1847, and was buried in Riverside Cemetery in Jackson, Tennessee.

Billy Blount followed in his father's footsteps, seeking a political career in the Knoxville area. Never marrying, he became the owner of the Blount Mansion in 1818. Prior to his death, he served as Secretary of the State of Tennessee; from 1816 to 1820, he also served as a member of the United States Congress. Dying on May 21, 1827, at the age of forty-three, he was buried in Paris, Tennessee.

Richard lived to be the oldest of the Blount children. When he died in 1858, he was seventy-seven years old. He and his brother

Billy had lived as wards of Willie Blount and Hugh Lawson White. In 1810, Richard married Catherine "Katy" Minor, moving to Montgomery County in Tennessee. Four children were born of that marriage.

Barbara Blount, Molsey's daughter, born in Knoxville September 16, 1792. Painted in 1952 by artist Mary Etta Grainger. Courtesy McClung Museum of Natural History and Culture, University of Tennessee, Knoxville.

The last son of Molsey and William died at the age of eighteen in 1809. Willie, as with Richard and Billy, had also cared for Jacob and ensured his future by sending him to the popular Virginia institution, William and Mary College. Jacob died while at college and is most likely buried nearby. He is not buried in the First Presbyterian Church Cemetery in Knoxville.

Upon the death of their mother, Barbara Blount went to live with her older sister, Louisa. Interestingly, she wed a man much like her father. Edmund Pendleton Gaines, a soldier, surveyor, and an Indian commissioner, became famous during the War of 1812, rising to the level of a Brigadier General by the time he met Barbara. By 1836 he was in command of the Southwest Military District, a job similar to her father's job in 1790. Barbara, married at the age of twenty-six in 1818, was his second wife. She died in Mobile, Alabama, in 1836, just as her husband assumed command of another military district. They had one child.

The last daughter and youngest child of Molsey and William was Eliza Indiana. She was seven years old when her mother died. Raised by her older sisters, Eliza met her future husband while living with Louisa and Pleasant Miller. In 1816, at the age of twenty-one, she married Edwin Wiatt, Pleasant Miller's nephew. History has confused his last name, listing him as Wiatt or Wyatt in different genealogical entries. Wiatt served as a United States Army surgeon. He and Eliza had three children. Eliza died in La Grange, Tennessee, in 1835 at the age of forty.

Several Blount relatives are buried in the First Presbyterian Church Cemetery in Knoxville. William Blount was the first, Molsey the third, to be buried on the designated land donated by James White for a future church and cemetery. Three years after Molsey's death, her sister-in-law, Ann Harvey, died in Knoxville on June 3, 1805. Ann had escorted Nancy from Tarborough after the death of William, staying on to keep Molsey company. Ann never returned to North Carolina, taking her role as aunt to William's children seriously.

The remains of Blount Wiatt (as spelled on his gravestone), a three-month-old child who died on December 18, 1820, lies beside Ann Harvey in the cemetery. He was probably the firstborn son of the Blount's daughter, Eliza Blount Wiatt. The Wiatts lived in Knoxville until they moved to LaGrange, Tennessee, near Memphis.

First Presbyterian Church and cemetery. When Molsey was buried, only two other graves were present and there was not a church building in 1800.

The legacy of the Blounts has continued through the lingering tales about William Blount in the echoes inside Blount Mansion and the questions their lives provoked. The worth and words of William Blount have been debated for centuries. Very little has been noted about the life and actions of Molsey Blount until now. Hopefully, this story will cause others to search deeper into the life of an incredible First Lady.

Conclusion

Molsey Blount's early death stunned both her family and community. Leaving behind her young children, who became orphans, was the worst of it. Molsey had survived so many losses and tragedies, had cared for all nine of her babies, buried two children, and loved a political titan who seemed more fascinated with power and wealth than with his wife and family. Perhaps her sudden death released her from further loss and grief. At the very least, it relieved her of the burdens of the tragedies she had borne for so long.

Born during a time when women were disenfranchised and silenced, she appears then disappears in the annals of colonial history. Her voice is silenced, her ideas lost, and her movements commented on occasionally by relatives, mostly those of her husband's. Oh, to meet this woman and ask her the questions lingering after the research and writing of this biography. What really happened to your firstborn son, Cornelius? Why didn't your older girls live with you as children? Was your marriage lonely, or was it fulfilling? After your carriage accident, what really kept you in North Carolina? Which place do you consider to be your real home—North Carolina or Tennessee? The questions are endless. Perhaps future historians will answer them, or perhaps they are always meant to confound us.

For now, we are left with an incomplete yet reputable understanding of this colonial First Lady's life. The temptation is to measure her life by the standard of a twenty-first-century woman's experience. The liberated, self-empowered, bra-burning individual may view Molsey as helpless or subservient to her husband. The tendency to categorize her as only a wife, mother, and household organizer is an error that must be avoided at all cost. Though her roles were shaped by society's expectations of a woman and wife, the colonial experiences also direct us to consider her as a self-confident and exceptionally strong person, living through adversity and despair. Yet we never hear directly from Molsey. She definitely fulfilled her role as a wife to a political titan. But what was she really like?

Honed in the crucible of the Revolutionary War and married to an errant political husband, Molsey Blount emerged determined to stand her ground in the face of threatening Indian attacks, childhood diseases, loss, tragedy, loneliness, and, yes, her husband's dogged focus on anything but her and their children. And the historical record is silent regarding her responses to these challenges: preferring to focus on her beauty and her strength. Under her care and watchful eye, her husband was supported in his reach for notoriety and wealth. Excluded from monetary decisions that ultimately caused the loss of her home, she managed to keep her scattered family together until her death. All through her married life, she endured the hardships and responsibilities of a plantation wife and eventually participated in the subduing of the frontier of Knoxville. It was her ease with social graces that calmed the Cherokee visitors to the mansion and her graceful presence that promoted Knoxville's entrance into the arena of a tamed and socially accepted frontier town.

Molsey remained an example of an educated and spirited colonial First Lady. Though she would probably be astonished to find herself described in this manner, she stands as somewhat of a celebrity, especially in today's standards. She knew she was married to a celebratory public figure and that her children would follow in the political footsteps of their father, but she would have denied this status for herself. Yet surely she would be interested in setting the record straight and having history complete the story of a powerful man's wife and premier First Lady.

Though we cannot look at her life through the lens of our current culture, customs, social norms, and behaviors between men and women, we can consider her feelings. As all human beings experience feelings of love, hate, loss, pain, frustration, loneliness, etc., Molsey was no exception. An honest look at her life would include these powerful complications to what appears to be a "normal" colonial woman's experience. If that suggestion is accepted, a new means of understanding her life emerges.

On the outside, historians may find a self-confident, strong governor's wife. I suggest that the veneer of that life was underscored and eroded by her struggles with loneliness, abandonment, and death. As Molsey is revealed through the words of others in this biography, her true personality is obscured by the propriety of colonial verse. One complication that is noted in this light is the possibility of debilitating depression.

Early in her saga, we learn of a strange loss. Subsequent to the death of her firstborn son, she soon delivers two more children—two girls found living with relatives, not with her. Why would a healthy, loving mother give her two children to another to raise, especially after the death of her firstborn? Such a loss would surely lead to depression, if not to at least sadness and dismay.

Another irony in her life was her continual practice of leaving behind her children even as she attempted to keep the family together. Often in her story, Molsey was reported to travel back and forth between her homeland North Carolina and Knoxville. On each trip, she ended up with her youngest or oldest children being left on either side of the mountains. As a colonial mother who loved her children, these long absences are confounding. Following her political husband and leaving the children behind became the hallmark of her life. The emotional life of this colonial mother becomes worrisome.

Molsey's carriage accident spawns other questionable events concerning her well-being. She was away from five of her children for over a year and a half. After the accident William visited her for a short period of time on his return to Knoxville from North Carolina. A year later, this narcissistic husband did not attempt to bring her home, or even to visit her. When Molsey finally returned to Knoxville, it appeared their marriage has cooled. From 1795 until William's death in March of 1800, she bore no more children. She was only thirty-four years old in 1795, an age in which women were still having children. If it was true their marriage had cooled, Molsey's feelings would have been a mixture of loathing, disappointment, relief, and maybe even disgust. There is also the possibility that the accident left her scarred, depressed, or incapacitated.

Molsey's death ended whatever was really happening to this lady. She most likely welcomed death, as the earlier death of William had left her at the mercy of brothers-in-law and without control of her children's future. The illness leading up to her death would have been tortuously slow, another cause for depression and despair, yet most assuredly her children were there during her last moments.

Lastly, one must ask the inevitable question: how often did feelings of love and warmth appear in the Blount marriage? Without any response from Molsey, we are left with only William's singular verse—"my dear Molsey"— stated in relation to her accident. Unfortunately, this sole entry by William leaves historians wondering about the obvious lack of affectionate words. Often it is easier to imagine or extrapolate that love was central to this marriage.

It is preferable to think of Molsey as having gained some sense of autonomy in her marriage to William Blount since her story often turns to self-determination and survival. Overcoming adversity and discontent bestowed on her the position similar to other American colonial women such as Abigail Adams or Mary Jemison. So it is that Molsey became a unique combination of resolve and resilience, malleability and mystery.

While important historical characters have continued to wind their way into the dialogue of America's past, Molsey Blount has become a part of that discussion. Her legacy, her life, and her children have become a part of the national consciousness and now part and parcel of the fabric of the State of Tennessee's foundation. Brought from behind the shadows of her political husband, Molsey Blount now stands on her own as the premier First Lady of Tennessee.

Bibliography

Block, S. T., and F. L. Block. *The Wrights of Wilmington.* Wilmington, North Carolina: S. Block, 1992.

Blount, B. *Blount Family Papers.* Raleigh: North Carolina State Archives, 1980.

Blount, W. *Blount Mansion Interpreter's Manual.* Blount Mansion Association. N.p.: Knoxville, 1997.

Blount, W. *Correspondence of William Blount, 1749–1800.* Knoxville: Knox County Archives, Microfilm B1–F1, 1933.

Blount, W. *Letters of William Blount 1790–1796.* Knoxville: Unknown.

Blount, W. William Blount Rodman Papers. East Carolina Manuscript Collection.

Carson, C. *Beginning of the Republic 1775–1825.* Wadley: American Textbook Committee, 1984.

"Childbirth in Early America." *Digital History, University of Houston.* Accessed April 22, 2013. http://www.digitalhistory.uh.edu/topic_display.cfm?tcid=70

Cluett, J. "Open Fractures: Injuries to the Bone with Associated Soft tissue and Skin Damage." *Orthopedics: About.com.* Accessed July 22, 2013. http://orthopedics.about.com/cs/brokenbones/g/openfracture.htm (site discontinued).

Cobb, Rev. P. L. "William Cobb—Host of Gov. William Blount." *Tennessee Historical Magazine* 9, no. 4 (1926): 1–24.

Demos, J. "Husbands and Wives." In *Our American Sisters: Women in American Life and Thought*, edited by Jean Friedman and William Shade, 24–37. Boston: Allyn and Bacon Inc., 1973.

Drane, R. *Historical Notices of St. James Episcopal Church.*
Philadelphia: R. S. H. George, 1843.

Dunklee, E, K. Hinder, J. Pollock, E. Voss, and S. Williams.
"Gender & Sexuality in Colonial America." *Gettysburg College.*
Accessed April 27, 2013. http://public.gettysburg.edu/
~tshannon/341/sites/Gender%20and%20Sexuality/Gender%20
Roles.htm.

Durham, W. T. *Before Tennessee: The Southwest Territory, 1790–
1796: A Narrative History of the Territory of the United States
South of the River Ohio.* Piney Flats, Tennessee: Rocky Mount
Historical Association, 1990.

Earle, A. *Home and Child Life in Colonial Days,* edited by Shirley
Glubok. Toronto: The Macmillan Company, 1969.

Fischer, K. *Suspect Relations: Sex, Race, and Resistance in Colonial
North Carolina.* Ithaca: Cornell University Press, 2002.

Fisher, R. H. "Biographical Sketches of Wilmington Citizens."
East Carolina University Digital Collections. Wilmington:
Wilmington Stamp and Printing, 1929. Accessed June 10,
2013. http://digital.lib.ecu.edu/17092.

Folmsbee, S. and S. Dillon. "The Blount Mansion: Tennessee's
Territorial Capitol." *Tennessee Historical Quarterly* 22 (1963):
106–129.

Fonvielle, C. E. *Historic Wilmington & the Lower Cape Fear: An
Illustrated History.* San Antonio: Historical Pub Network,
2007.

Friedman, J., and W. Shade, *Our American Sisters.* Boston: Allyn
and Bacon Inc, 1973.

Gardner, A. "Courtship, Sex, and the Single Colonist: The
Colonial Williamsburg Official History & Citizenship Site."
Colonial Williamsburg. Accessed July 4, 2013.

http://www.history.org/foundation/journal/holiday07/court.cfm.

Glubok, S. *Home and Child Life in Colonial Days.* Toronto: The Macmillan Company, 1969.

Godbeer, R. "Sexual Revolution in Early America." Baltimore: Johns Hopkins University Press, 2002. Accessed September 3, 2013. http://web.campbell.edu/faculty/vandergriff/FamColonial.html.

Grainger, C. *Last Will and Testament, 1765.* Accessed September 10, 2013. http://www.ncgenweb.us/newhanover/cgrainger.html

Grainger, C. *Grainger Family Genealogy.* N.p.: Wilmington, 2013.

Greene, E. "Pregnancy and Childbirth for the Historical Author." Elenagreene.com. Accessed July 9, 2013. http://www.elenagreene.com/childbirth.html.

Hale, P. *Colonial Records of North Carolina.* Raleigh: North Carolina, 1886.

Hamer, P. "Letters of Gov. William Blount: 1790–1796." *Journal of East Tennessee Historical Society* 4 (1932): 122–137.

Hellier, C. "Physical, Intellectual, Biographical: Our Ideas of Privacy and Their Evolution." *Colonial Williamsburg* (2013): 48–54.

Hewlett, C. W. and M. Smalley. *Between the Creeks: A History of Masonborough Sound, 1735–1970.* Wilmington, NC: Wilmington Print Co., 1971.

"History of Birth Control Methods." New York: Katherine Dexter McCormick Library and Planned Parenthood Federation of America, 2006.

"History of St. James Episcopal Church." *St. James Episcopal Church.* Accessed October 10, 2013.

http://www.ecva.org/congregations/features/
st_james_wilmington/st_james_wilmington.pdf.

Hood, D. F. *Historic Architecture of New Hanover County, North Carolina.* Wilmington, North Carolina: The New Hanover County Planning Department, 1986. Accessed January 2, 2014. http://laserfiche.nhcgov.com/weblink/0/edoc/3273630/Historic-Architecture-of-NHC.pdf

Hymowitz, C. and M. Weissman. *A History of Women in America.* New York: Bantam Books, 1978.

Kammerer, R. "Yours If You Came." *Glimpse, 2012.* Accessed May 20, 2013. http://visitgreenvillenc.com/about-us/about-greenville-pitt-county/history-of-greenville/

Keith, A., editor. *The John Gray Blount Papers.* vol. 1 (1764–1789) and 2 (1790–1795). Winston-Salem: Winston Printing Company, 1952.

Kellam, I. St. *James Church Historical Record 1737–1852.* Wilmington: unknown, 1965.

King, H. *Sketches of Pitt County: A Brief History of County 1704–1910.* Raleigh: Edwards & Broughton Printing Company, 1911.

Lennon, D., and I. Kellam. *The Wilmington Town Book.* Raleigh: Department of Cultural Resources, 1973.

Lewis, L. *The Lower Cape Fear in Colonial Days.* Chapel Hill: University of North Carolina Press, 1965.

Lucas, P. R. *American Odyssey, 1607–1789.* Englewood Cliffs: Prentice-Hall, 1984.

Masterson, W. *William Blount.* Baton Rouge: Louisiana State University Press, 1954.

Masterson, W., editor. *The John Gray Blount Papers,* vol. 3 (1796–1802). Raleigh: State Department of Archives and History, 1965.

McArthur, W. "Knoxville's History: An Interpretation." *Heart of the Valley,* edited by Lucile Deaderick. Knoxville: East Tennessee Historical Society, 1976.

McKenney, J. *Women of the Constitution: Wives of the Signers.* Toronto: The Scarecrow Press, Inc., 2013.

McKoy, E. *Early Wilmington: Block by Block from 1733 On.* N.p.: Wilmington, 1967.

Mintz, S., "Mothers and Fathers in America: Looking Backward, Looking Forward." *Digital History–University of Houston.* Accessed July 9, 2013.

Morris, E. "Topographical Dictionary." In *The Tennessee Gazetteer,* 30–37. Nashville, 1834.

Norton, H. *Religion in Tennessee 1777–1945.* Knoxville: University of Tennessee Press, 1981.

Norton, M. B. *Liberty's Daughters: The Revolutionary Experience of American Women, 1750–1800.* Boston: Little, Brown and Company, 1980.

"Obituary of Col. Jacob Blount 1789." USGenWeb. Accessed October 22, 2013. https://www.geni.com/people/Col-Jacob-Blount/6000000002183092924.

Olmert, M. Longinus. "On the Sublime What Everyone Read." *Colonial Williamsburg.* Winter 2013, 43–48.

Pharaoh Lee Cobb Microfilm: 1866–1957 (Documentary). Directed by Cobb. USA: Pharaoh Cobb Family, 1960.

Philippe, L. *Diary of My Travels in America.* New York: Delacorte Press, 1977.

Phillips, P. "Never a Safe Road: Postal Communications in the Southwest Territory." *Journal of East Tennessee History* 62 (1990): 18–32.

Pitt County Development Commission. "Economic History of Pitt County 1690–2012." *Pitt County.* Accessed June 4, 2013. http://www.locateincarolina.com/wp-content/uploads/2010/06/Economic-History-of-Pitt-County-October-20121.pdf.

Powell, W. S. *North Carolina: A History.* Chapel Hill: University of North Carolina Press, 1988.

Ramsey, JGM. *The Annals of Tennessee.* Charleston: John Russell, 1853.

Reaves, B. *Southport (Smithville): A Chronology.* Wilmington: Broadfoot Publishing Company, 1978.

Rocky Mount Christmas 1791: The Arrival of Governor Blount and His Family. Piney Flats: Rocky Mount Museum, n.d.

"Rocky Mount: Where History Comes Alive." *Rocky Mount Museum.* Piney Flats: Rocky Mount Museum, n.d.

Roultiere, G. *Knoxville Gazette.* Rogersville: G. Roultiere, 1793.

Saunders, William. *Colonial Records of North Carolina, Volume 10.* N.p.: Raleigh, 1886.

Sevier, J. *Diary of John Sevier*, edited by John H. DeWitt. Accessed July 12, 2013. http://penelope.uchicago.edu/Thayer/E/Gazetteer/People/John_Sevier/Journal/home.html.

Smith, D. *The Blount Journal, 1790–1796.* Nashville: Benson Printing Company, 1955.

Smith, E. "Compleat Housewife or Accomplish'd Gentlewoman's Companion." Accessed June 22, 2013. http://www.nationalhumanitiescenter.org/pds/becomingamer/ideas/text7/homemedicalguides.pdf.

Spruill, J. "Participation in Public Affairs." In *Our American Sisters: Women in American Life and Thought*, 38–51. Edited by Jean Friedman and William Shade. Boston: Allyn and Bacon Inc., 1973.

Sprunt, J. *Chronicles of the Cape Fear River: Being Some Account of Historic Events on the Cape Fear River*. Raleigh: Edwards & Broughton Printing Company, 1914.

Thorne, B. *The Heritage of Craven County North Carolina*. Winston-Salem: Hunter Publishing Company, 1984.

Waddell, A. *History of New Hanover County and the Lower Cape Fear Region, 1723–2800: Volume 1*. N.p.: Wilmington, 1909.

Walser, R. "Thomas Godfrey Jr., NCpedia." *NCpedia*. Accessed June 2, 2013. http://ncpedia.org/biography/godfrey-thomas-jr.

Wertz, R. and D. Wertz. *Lying-In: A History of Childbirth in America*. London: Yale University Press, 1977.

Whaley, H. "Colonial Midwifery." *Wonders and Marvels*. Accessed July 9, 2013. http://wondersandmarvels.com/2011/06/colonial-midwifery.html.

Whitworth, K. "Blount Mansion: Parking Lot or Landmark." *East Tennessee Historical Journal*, 62 (1990): 80–92.

William Blount: The Man and His Mansion. Knoxville: Blount Mansion Association, 1977.

Wood, L. M. "Marriage in Colonial North Carolina." North Carolina Digital Library. Accessed October 10, 2013. http://www.learnnc.org/lp/editions/nchist-colonial/4079.

Wright, L. *Life in Colonial America*. New York: Capricorn Books, 1965.

Wright, M. *Some Account of the Life and Services of William Blount*. Washington: E. J. Gray Publishers, 1884.

Index

227

69299376R00126

Made in the USA
Columbia, SC
15 August 2019